BOLOGNESE COOKING HERITAGE

BARBARA BERTUZZI

BOLOGNESE COOKING HERITAGE

 Pendragon

Barbara Bertuzzi
Bolognese Cooking Heritage
The recipes of the "Vecchia Scuola"

Design: Studio GI&I
Editing by Isabella Neri and Simone Buttazzi
Traslation by Pierluigi Guidi

This book was supported by:

Dept. for the Environment and Territory Protection
Province di Bologna, Dept. for Tourism
Bologna Tourism

 Ergap – Environment Service

A publication under the aegis of:

Comune di Bologna
Dept. for the Productive,
Commercial and Tourism activities

Regione Emilia-Romagna
Dept. for Commerce and Tourism

Index

7   Introduction

9   The Vecchia Scuola Bolognese

12   The pastry

19   Simple pasta

24   Filled pasta

28   Home-made bread

33   Bolognese-style mixed fry, sweet and savory

50   Starters, appetisers and snacks

67   Fresh pasta dishes

85   Fillings for all kinds of filled pasta

90   Sauces and seasonings

105   Soups and broth

113   Meat-based second courses

127   Side dishes and more

141   Fish-based second courses

144   Cheese

147   Soups and broth

160   Cakes

181   Tasty delights

191   Fruit in syrup and jams, liquors and hot beverages

201   Alfabetical index of the recipes

Introduction

Bolognese cooking heritage is not just a recipe book but a real cooking handbook. Its aim is not to fill an empty space on your bookshelves but to live in your kitchen, among the household appliances. But most of all it needs to be used, over and over again, until its pages are torn, or yellowed with time, or even – why not? – stained with some sauce!

Bolognese cooking heritage has been written to be used especially by those who are beginners in the kitchen, but also by kitchen experts. One page after the other, everybody will learn about traditional Bolognese dishes in depth as well as some modern versions, and then be able to prepare them in an old-fashioned way: respecting the seasons and preferring fresh and typical products, learning to cook not only the quantity of food needed daily, but also something more to be stored and served later.

Our recipes will not tell you the preparation time of a dish, but will give you plenty of advice on how to cook it, even in different stages... Even the most elaborate dishes can be easy, if the preparation is well organized. Thus, you can optimize time. So, two or three servings of fresh egg pasta, perfectly seasoned, can be prepared in just a few minutes if our freezer includes some sauce and some pasta, made with our own hands during one of those relaxing moments we take for ourselves, to knead the dough and roll out the pastry. It is not that difficult to imagine. Cooking, by the way, has always been a good diversion.

Dear readers, or rather, dear users of this book: it's time to go back to cooking with passion.

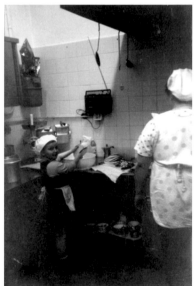

The typical product of the Park

Through the pages of this handbook, we will introduce you to some typical products while you will find them listed among the ingredients of our recipes.
What is a typical product?
First of all, in order to be included in this category, it should fulfill some territory, tradition and genuineness requirements.
Slow Food, appointed by the *Ministero dell'Ambiente and Tutela del Territorio* (Dept. for the Environment and Territorial protection) and in co-operation with Ferderparchi and Legambiente (environment associations), has created the first *Atlante dei prodotti tipici dei parchi italiani* (Atlas of the typical products of Italian parks), listing only those traditional country productions, resulting from the work of many artisans all over the Italian territory who still work according to the traditions handed down by local farmers.
This is a way to increase the value of the agricultural and food industry.
For this reason, the list does not include those companies that process cold meats with lactose, saccharose or ascorbic acid or that use additives for cheeses or make bread with chemical yeast instead of "mother" yeast. During this two-year research for the *Atlas*, the Slow Food experts have interviewed farmers, shepherds and butchers of the protected areas all over Italy, tasting all their products and enjoying this marriage between environment and food.
The products we will mention are the typical products of the only National Park in Emilia Romagna, near Bologna: the National Park of *Foreste casentinesi, Monte Falterona, Campigna*.

Key

Level of difficulty of the recipes
The level of difficulty of each recipe is expressed with reference to its preparation:

✳ easiest dishes, suitable also for kitchen beginners

✳ ✳ dishes that require a little more care and experience

✳ ✳ ✳ more elaborate dishes, not suitable for kitchen beginners

The Vecchia Scuola Bolognese

This is a journey through the world of taste and genuine products of emilian land. The traditions of a city that is known for its millenary food culture give birth to a meeting and training point addressed to foreigners and local people.

At the *Vecchia Scuola Bolognese* everybody can discover or re-discover the taste of the typical home-made cooking, go through the "habits and customs" of long and labored food preparations that, not long ago, involved our mothers, aunts and grand-mothers in preparing historic dishes that are now famous all over the world. Nowadays, those traditions have mostly been forgotten, yet young generations still wish to learn some recipes, testing themselves in front of the cooker.

This is much more than just a school: this exciting place feels like home. It is a chance to meet real good food and, most of all, to experience the *bolognesità*, which is a mix of the characteristics of the town and its inhabitants: hospitality, brotherhood mixed with solidarity and a great amount of passion for genuineness, with a dash of restlessness.

The *Vecchia Scuola Bolognese* guards the old taste of traditional Petronian recipes by uniting the history of local gastronomy to the improvement of the territory.

When visiting the school, located in the city centre, the most striking thing is the great number of people coming and going: on the one hand, students ready for their lessons on fresh pasta, standing in front of the board and holding their rolling-pins. On the other hand, people who got here to taste a real *bolognese* dish, watching the art of kneading and the finishing of *tortellini, tortelloni, tagliatelle* and *lasagne* from behind the glass wall that separates the restaurant area from the laboratory. Those who drop by in the afternoon can taste a freshly baked sweet in a comfortable but unusual ambience.

What are the origins of this heaven of aromas and perfumes? It is a family tradition. Alessandra Spisni, the owner, had the insight to revive in the third millennium what once was ordinary and usual

and that today can still be appreciated by the most demanding and refined gourmets. This is how simple home-made dishes become extraordinarily amazing: some are rich in succulent ingredients, some others are simpler and the result of the need of having all the family around the dining table with very tasty country food in hard times.

The *Vecchia Scuola Bolognese* teaches how to recognize the genuine taste of good cooking and how to recreate the rituality of a way of cooking that has been disregarded for too long. Alessandra cannot remember when she started rolling out the pastry, she was too young. The same can be said by her daughter, Stefania, who plays an active role in the company as well. Once, all the families used to do this: everyday, pasta was homemade and the technique was handed down naturally from generation to generation. Nowadays, things are not like that anymore. Many people have not even seen anyone making it, many others cannot tell fresh handmade pasta from that pasta processed and rolled-out by a machine.

Sfogline and sfoglini...

Not everybody knows who the *sfogline* or the *sfoglini* are. Yes, because they can be both men and women. The name identifies those people who, starting from handmade pastry, can propose traditional dishes such as *tortellini* and *tagliatelle*, as well as more modern dishes, such as the chestnut and *ricotta tortelli* and the *strichetti*.

Some were born *sfoglina*, like Alessandra Spisni, but most of them chose to become one. There are those who start for fun, continue for passion and end up with a new profession. There are those who, and they are many, start as a hobby and continue because it is relaxing and lets them forget about daily matters. Finally, there are those who become enthusiastic about it and love to practice this art, preparing delicious dishes at home.

At the *Vecchia Scuola Bolognese* you can meet not only housewives who want to improve their food knowledge, but also people who have other jobs and, instead of going to the gym at night, prefer becoming a *sfoglino* or a *sfoglina*…

Italian and foreign hotel personnel is trained at the *Vecchia Scuola Bolognese*. Every year, tourists and students come from abroad to spend some special days here and to attend the demonstrations given by Alessandro, the owner's brother, who is also in charge of the organization and the syllabus of the courses.

Each course is customized. The students decide by themselves how deep they want to go into the subject. Moreover, the students and teachers are always in touch: students can call and ask for advice on the use of new ingredients; they compare their experiences in order to try new variations; they become the very best "clients", as they grow fond of genuine tastes and come back to find them!

↑ The whole staff of The Vecchia Scuola Bolognese: from the left Alessandro Spisni, Renzo Canalicchio, Alessandra Spisni, Stefania Canalicchio, Daniela Biancu and Damiano Greto.

The pastry

The pastry is made of eggs and flour. In average, 1 egg per 100 g of flour, although this is quite an approximate quantity as eggs are not always the same: the external shell and the white inside can vary. Moreover, flour can have a different humidity rate, which can differ from type to type. All these factors can affect the result of the dough we are about to make.

The art of pastry is acquired through familiarity and practice: it is important to feel it in our hands, process it until we are able to see if it is too soft – and then add a little flour, gradually – or too hard – adding another egg or just the white if necessary. Never add water: it would only be a palliative, as it would create instant humidity without providing the necessary elasticity.

Adding an egg white, on the other hand, improves the consistency of the dough as it does not evaporate easily. Sometimes, you just need to get your hands wet and start processing the dough again to give it the necessary humidity.

The pastry technique

The dough

As a start, make a wide flour well in the middle of the board, around 20-30 cm diameter. Shell the eggs into the hole in the middle of the well. Use a fork to scramble the eggs and to stir them slowly, giving them time to absorb the flour and paying attention not to break the borders wasting all the egg on the board.

↑↓   Pastry preparation.

Slowly, the flour mixes with the eggs and the mix gets thicker. This is when we can check if the quantities are correct, otherwise we can add an egg or some more flour.

When the dough becomes consistent enough, you can start processing it: stir it, gradually giving it elasticity by means of your hands' warmth and harmonious movements. Handle it with both hands, lifting it up with your fingers and pressing it forwards with your palms, without crushing or tearing it. After every move, turn it upside down and repeat.

The dough should not be too soft nor too hard; it should be soft and elastic, and most of all it must not stick to the board. The more you process it, the more you should feel its softness and elasticity; at the same time, the small, crackling air bubbles that are created inside the dough give it flexibility. This stage is essential for achieving a good pastry sheet.

After kneading for about 15-20 minutes, you get a thick dough. It is ready for rolling out when it is smooth, porous, elastic and lump-free.

It is important to leave it to rest for at least 10-15 minutes, protected from the air. You can cover it with a plate or close it in a nylon bag, so it becomes even softer. The more it rests, the easier the rolling out will be.

Rolling out the dough with the rolling pin

Right before rolling out the dough, if you notice that it is almost rock hard you are still in time to make it better! Make a small flour well on the border of the board with 50 g of flour and add 1 egg, with the usual kneading technique. After mixing it properly, add it to the first dough.

On the other hand, if the dough is flabby (this can happen also due to increased humidity in the air), before rolling it out, you should add as much flour as necessary. In fact, as long as the dough is not rolled out yet, it can easily absorb the added flour.

Once you have checked its consistency, cut the dough into as many pieces as it is required to make the pasta you want.

Now it is time to roll it out on the board: use your hands to make the dough into a ball, a round and very smooth one, which must not be crushed or torn. This is one of the most difficult things for beginners.

Put the ball in the middle of the board and press it down with the rolling pin, after dusting it with much flour. Now, keeping your hands parallel, pull the rolling pin from the middle outwards, letting it slide and pressing with your palms. At the beginning, it is advisable to press with energy in order to decrease the volume of the dough and make the processing quicker, keeping the dough from drying, which would affect the rest of the process.

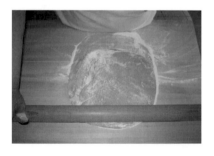

Repeat this movement with the rolling pin twice and then turn the dough upside down. Repeat twice more and then turn it upside down again, and so on, always following the same direction, either clockwise or anticlockwise. Complete the cycle at least twice, adding flour every now and then to the dough or on the board, never on the rolling pin. Add flour in very small quantities, just a light dusting, or it will not be absorbed.

As the pastry gets thinner, change the position of the hands on the rolling pin. At the beginning, the hands were equally distant, as the elbows made a right angle alongside the body, and the they pressed on the rolling pin as it slid. As the pastry gets thinner, the hands go outwards on the rolling pin and therefore the elbows move away from the body. For this reason, the gradual and soft movement of the hands

towards the centre of the rolling pin helps it slide and allows the pastry to become even and smooth. Now, you have to decrease the pressure on the rolling pin, otherwise you may spoil it.

It is advisable to turn from one side to the other and repeat the same movement with the rolling pin, rotating it often. A constant rotation of the pastry makes it easier to make it more regular and round, evenly thin.

Thus, the pastry becomes gradually larger and about 1/2 cm thick. Now you can take the pastry with your hands and lay it on the border of the lower part of the board, leaving a part of it on the outside and the other part in the middle of the board: this way you can keep the pastry while rolling it out. Then, from the middle of the pastry sheet, move the rolling pin forward towards the middle of the board, with a soft and constant touch, slowly stretching and rolling out the pastry. Turn it upside down and repeat. This way you will change its shape from round to stretched out.

The pastry becomes thinner and thinner. From this point on, it is advisable to roll it on the rolling pin, avoiding to touch it too much with your hands or it gets too dry. Complete the cycle, always in the same direction, and add flour if necessary.

As it gets longer, it becomes more difficult to roll it out. Do not keep on going from the middle of the pastry outwards because this could create creases and tear the pastry. On the other hand, process it near its borders, checking the spots where it is thicker and flattening it more and more.

Keep on making it evenly thin without rolling out the same point many times. Only two movements and then turn it. Two movements and then turn it. You reach the final stage when you get the thinness required for the type of pasta you want to make.

The right thinness

A generally thicker pastry, usually made by beginners, is perfect for all *ricotta*-stuffed pasta like *tortelloni, ravioli, caramelle, triangoli, mezzelune, pollicioni* and *cestini*. In fact, it has to be strong enough to keep the delicate filling while cooking.

This is not the case of *tortellini*. In fact, although they are stuffed, their filling does not release humidity, which can lead the pastry to break while cooking. Thus, its pastry is very thin (as tissue-paper, some say). It is very difficult to make it: it must stay smooth and it needs to be rolled out quickly, otherwise it loses its freshness and becomes difficult to seal. The same thinness is required for making *sorpresine*. However, the thinnest pastry is the one used for making the typical Carnival *sfrappole*!

On the other hand, *balanzoni*, with their tasty filling, require a strong pastry, like the one used for pasta stuffed with potatoes or with red turnips or the green pastry for *lasagne*.

On the contrary, if you want to make good *tagliatelle*, the pastry should not be too smooth. In this case, it is not necessary to leave the dough to rest and it can be rolled out straight away (it is actually advised). So the pastry stays firm and rough enough. As for thickness, it depends on personal taste. In Bologna it is usually quite thin whereas in other areas in Italy it is thicker. The pastry for *garganelli* and for *strichetti* is medium thin as well.

Cutting the pastry

Before cutting the pastry for any kind of pasta, it is necessary to keep it still on the board and move it with the hands, with the aid of the rolling pin. This way, you will be able to let all the air go out. If you do not perform this stage, the pastry would shrink after being cut, making all the types of pasta not the same.

Every kind of pasta, simple and stuffed, except for *tagliatelle*, is cut pressing only the tip of the rectangular kitchen knife on the pastry, holding it like a fountain pen.

On the other hand, when making *tagliatelle*, the kitchen knife should be held normally; never lift it from the board but let it slide forward, making it cut the pastry into parallel strips.

The colors of the pastry

Since its origins, people have worked out many variations to the pastry, which changed its color in accordance with the ingredients added to the dough. Thus, the green pastry, with spinach or nettle leaves; the red one, flavored with tomato; the yellow one, with saffron; the black one, colored with sepia; the brown one, with cocoa or with chestnut flour; and, finally, the "*prezzemolata*", with parsley. Many different kinds of pastry that go beyond the ancient Bolognese traditions.

Green: let's take into consideration a basic dough of 10 eggs and 1 kg of flour, according to the above-illustrated technique. In order to get good dough, it is advisable to always use at least 10 eggs: the exceeding dough can be stored in the fridge, covered.

If you want to make green pastry, you use one egg less and keep the same amount of flour. Add 70-80 g spinach, boiled in salted water, strained, cold hand-strained, and finely chopped with a knife. Remember that frozen spinach give more color, so use a smaller quantity. You can get the same color adding nettle leaves: they are less colored than spinach but give an intense perfume to the pastry.

If you want to use only 5 eggs, you cannot take away a whole egg but add as much flour as required by the process.

Red: to make red pastry, you can follow the same process. Just replace 1 egg with 70-80 g of tomato concentrate, adding it to the mix of 9 eggs and 1 kg of flour.

Yellow: it is achieved with saffron. Use the desired quantity of this Easter spice, adding it to the eggs and flour until you get the color you want, as well as the saffron flavor you want to give to your pastry.

> **Don't forget ...**
>
> **The board has two faces**
> Traditional pastry is prepared always on the same side of the board. On the other hand, we suggest using the other side of the board when making colored pastry with sepia, saffron, tomato paste or cocoa. So you will keep one side of the board clean and dedicate the other to the preparation of all kinds of colored fresh pasta.

↑ Ingredients for the green pastry.

↑ Ingredients for the red pastry.

↑ Ingredients for the yellow pastry.

↑ Ingredients for the black pastry.

↑ Ingredients for the brown pastry.

↑ Ingredients for the "Prezzemolata" pastry.

Black: this color is achieved with sepia, which is today sold in shops and is extracted by fresh cuttlefish. As well as giving this peculiar color, it also features great flavoring qualities. While processing 10 eggs and 1 kg of flour, add the right quantity of this liquid: in this case, not more than two packets.

Brown: brown pastry is achieved adding an unusual ingredient for egg pasta, that is cocoa. Mix 1 kg of flour with 11 eggs and add 100 g of bitter cocoa.

With chestnut flour: in this case, as well as wheat flour, we use chestnut flour. For example, add 700 g of wheat flour and 300 g of chestnut flour to 10 eggs.

"Prezzemolata", with parsley: the easiest way to make this special pastry, is to add the desired quantity of fresh, chopped parsley to the dough. A tastier variant of this recipe includes adding parmesan cheese and chopped garlic and parsley. Add pepper as desired.

This pastry is suitable to prepare any kind of simple pasta but also the stuffed ones, such as *lasagne*. On the other hand, it is not recommended for filled pasta, because it could break while cooking and waste the filling. A delicious example are the *straccetti* with garlic and parsley, which can be served both with sauce and in a soup.

Simple pasta

Strichetti or farfalle

Lay the pastry on the board, and cut it into 3 cm wide strips and then into squares. In order to enhance the "butterfly" effect, decorate two opposite sides of the square with the pastry cutter. Keep your thumb at the centre of the square, pull the part on top with your forefinger; then keep your forefinger still – blocking the fold – and pull with your thumb from the opposite side, making the second fold. The central knot should not be too thick or it will be difficult to cook.

Garganelli

Cut the pastry into 3 cm squares, just like for *strichetti* or *farfalle* and let them slide on the specially provided tool, called *comb*, which furrows its surface. Then, close the *garganello* shaping it like a small macaroni. Let them dry on a platter.

Storage and cooking: *strichetti* and *garganelli* can be stored dry in the fridge, at least for 5 or 6 days, in plastic bags. The pasta should not be too dry when being cooked or it could break. Cook them in boiling, salted water and strain them when they come to the surface.

Gnocchi

Work the dough according to the appropriate ingredients needed to make potato, *ricotta* or chestnut flour *gnocchi*. Process the resulting dough, after being well blended, with your hands and then make it into two 2 cm thick cylinders. Use a knife to cut 1 cm wide pieces. Finish the *gnocchi* letting them slide on the "*comb*", to give them their furrowed look.

The quantities following in the recipes below are for 6 persons.

Potato *gnocchi*: first of all, boil 700 g of potatoes and mash them after the peling them. When they are still warm, add 70 g of parmesan cheese, 300 g of wheat flour, 1 egg, salt and nutmeg, while kneading on the board and carefully blending all the ingredients. It will then be divided into two cylinders to make *gnocchi*. The traditional sauce for these *gnocchi* is "butter and gold" (see recipe on page 92), but they can be dressed with vegetable sauce or with *bolognese* sauce with parmesan cheese and béchamel as well. The latter dressing is the so-called "pasticciato".

Chestnut flour *gnocchi*: the process is similar to the above-mentioned one. Boil 700 g of potatoes and mash them. Replace wheat flour with 300 g chestnut flour, which will give the *gnocchi* a pleasant sweetish flavor. Add 70 g of parmesan cheese, 1 egg, salt and nutmeg, while kneading on the board and carefully blending all the ingredients. It will then be divided into two cylinders to make *gnocchi*.

It is advisable to dress them with a strong sauce to make a contrast with the chestnut sweetish flavor. For example, a turnip tops sauce, an eggplants-based dressing (just fried with salt and pepper, without adding tomato), or a mushroom sauce.

Ricotta *gnocchi*: ricotta *gnocchi* can be of various colors, green, white, red, black or yellow. According to the desired color, mix different quantities of the basic ingredients (such as flour, ricotta, and parmesan cheese) and add the coloring ingredient.

To make *green gnocchi* mix 500 g of ricotta, 150 g of parmesan cheese, 250 g of flour, 100 g of spinach, 1 egg, salt and nutmeg. To make the same quantity of *white gnocchi* mix 700 g of ricotta, 200 g of parmesan cheese, 250 g of flour, 2 eggs and as much chopped parsley as will suffice. If you want to make *red gnocchi*, replace parsley with a tablespoon tomato concentrate and use 1 egg (instead of 2). As for *yellow gnocchi*, replace tomato with the desired amount of saffron, blended with 2 eggs. Finally, for *black gnocchi*, use sepia and 1 egg.

Grattini

The dough for this pasta is made with 8 eggs, 100 g of parmesan cheese, 500 g of semolina and 250 g of breadcrumbs. Mix the ingredients and work them according to the traditional pastry-making process. Once you make a big loaf, cut it into large pieces. Let the pieces dry for about 30 minutes and then grate them on the coarse side of the grater. Leave *grattini* to dry all night long.

↑   The Grattini grater.

Malfattini

Make an about 1/2 cm-thick pastry and leave it to rest until it is dry. Finally cut with a knife, making many small chunks until the pastry is almost ground.

Maltagliati

This name means that these pieces of pasta are not cut in the same way. They are mainly made with unused pieces of pastry without a specific shape.

Parpadellini or quadretti

This is a small kind of pasta used in soups. Cut the pastry in many thin strips, 4-5 mm wide, and then cut them across, making many small square-shaped pieces of pasta.

Storage and cooking: *maltagliati, parpadellini, malfattini* and *grattini* can be stored dry in the fridge in cellophane bags or in jars. You can cook them in boiling broth, vegetable or bean soup. Just remember to turn off the heat when they emerge.

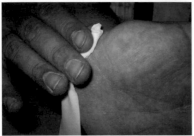

Strozzapreti

This is the only kind of traditional fresh pasta without eggs. The dough only consists of flour and water: 50 cl of water per 100 g of flour.

Knead the dough as usual and roll out a thick pastry, yet thinner than that used for *tortelloni*. Lay it on the board and cut it into 0,5 cm wide strips: then roll it in your hands (making your hands slide one against the other) to make *strozzapreti*. If necessary, you can moisten your hand-palms to work the pasta better.

Storage and cooking: *strozzapreti* can be stored in the freezer, not too dry. They cook quickly if they are fresh. On the other hand, when they are frozen, they need more time to cook.

Remove them from salted, boiling water as soon as they emerge. You can add some water while sautéing them in the frying pan to complete their cooking. Dress them with tasty sauces, sautéing them in the frying pan. Their spiral shape makes them perfect for vegetable or fish sauces.

Tagliatelle, pappardelle and taglioline

Tagliatelle are 7-8 mm wide pasta noodles: they are made by rolling the pastry on the board, making a multi-layer cylinder. After flattening it, without squashing it, use a wide-bladed knife to cut *tagliatelle* of the above-mentioned width, making many pasta rollers that will be lain on the board as small "*tagliatelle* nests".

In Bologna, they are typically served with *bolognese* sauce (see recipe on page 94). They can also be dressed with: ham sauce, also adding peas, and mushroom sauce, or, as in the most modern version, enriched with salmon for Christmas Eve dinner (see recipe on pages 96-98 and 101).

A variant of *tagliatella* is surely *pappardella*, which can be from 2 to 4 cm wide. If it is going to be dressed with mushrooms, it should be about 2 or 3

↑ Taglioline nest.

cm wide, whereas it can be around 3 to 4 cm wide if it is to be dressed with venison sauce.

The thinnest version, only 3 mm wide, is called *tagliolina*. It is perfect for stock, both chicken or vegetable. It can also be dressed in a more modern way with zucchini and crayfish or with a vegetable sauce. Both dressings are especially suitable in summer (recipe on page 101).

Storage and cooking: *tagliatelle*, *pappardelle* and *taglioline* can be stored in a fresh place but not in the fridge. First they should be made into "nests" in order to let air go through them, then dried, wrapped in paper and packed in cellophane bags.

Tagliatelle and *pappardelle* are best cooked "al dente". Plunge into boiling, salted water and strain when they emerge. Then dress with sauce, adding a few spoons of cooking water in order to keep the right humidity rate.

On the other hand, *taglioline* should be cooked in stock, vigorously boiling. Turn fire off when it starts boiling again. It is advisable not to cook more than 5 or 6 servings at a time.

↑ Tagliatelle.   Pappardelle. ↓

23

Filled pasta

All kinds of filled pasta (except for *tortellini*, which are filled with meat) need to be blanched before being stored. What does it mean? They need to be plunged, in small quantities, in boiling salted water and removed as soon as they come to the surface of the water. Let them dry and then put in cellophane bags. So they can be stored for some days in the fridge.

If the filling consists of fish or cheese, it is advisable to eat the pasta on the same day. *Tortellacci* should be eaten straight away as well. In fact, if they are frozen it is very difficult to cook them because their filling takes a long time to cook on account of their size, whereas the pastry gets cooked quickly.

You can tell that filled pasta is ready when it gets swollen and not, as many believe, when it comes to the surface of the water.

Balanzoni

They are typical green *tortelloni*, with a very rich filling: ricotta, spinach, basil, *mortadella*, parmesan cheese and nutmeg. The traditional recipe suggests to dress them with butter and sage (see recipe on page 67).

Caramelle

Cut the pastry with the pastry cutter, as if for *tortelloni*, into 6 cm squares. Fill them and close them, making a filled cylinder, leaving enough space at the sides to close them like a candy. The closing joint should not be too thick or it will not cook well.

Cestini

To make *cestini* cut the pastry into 6 cm squares. Fill them and close them on top, joining the two ends.

Mezzelune

Cut the pastry with a 6 cm diameter round cutter and fill them. Once the filling is in place, close the two half-circles, decorating the borders with your fingers.

Pollicioni

As for *ravioli*, put the filling on one half of the pastry. Use a 6 cm round mould on this half of the pastry to define the areas on which you will put the filling. Lay the other half of the pastry on it and cut the circles. Close them, so that the filling is in the centre.

Ravioli

Lay the pastry on the board and fold it. Put the filling on one half of the pastry, every 1.5 cm, leaving the same space on each side.

Lay the other half of the pastry on it and close *ravioli* one by one, following the lines created by the filling shape. Spray a little water, if necessary, to moisten the pastry in order to make it easier to close it. Finally, use the pastry cutter to decorate the sides of *ravioli*.

Triangoli

The process is the same as for *cestini*; the only difference is that, in this case, they should be closed in the shape of a triangle. Finish them decorating their sides with a pastry cutter or a fork.

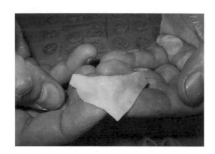

Tortellini

To make *tortellini*, also known as "Venus' belly buttons", lay the pastry on the board and use a cellophane sheet to cover the part you are not going to cut, in order to save its freshness. At this point, define the pasta strips using a knife or with the special cutter for *tortellini*, about 3 cm wide. Then cut every strip into squares.

Put, with your fingertips, a touch of filling on each square (see recipe on page 89). Close the square in a triangular shape, pressing firmly on both sides, and then wrap it around your forefinger to close the two ends.

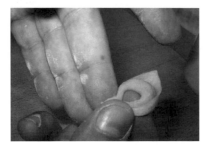

Lay *tortellini* on a platter, without overlaying them.

According to the traditional recipe, they should be cooked in chicken stock (see recipe on page 111).

Storage and cooking: *tortellini* can be stored in the fridge (or in the freezer) up to a week, after drying them thoroughly. Cook them in boiling stock, they are ready when they come to the surface. Let them rest 2 or 3 minutes before serving.

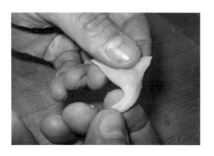

Did you know?

The "poor" version of tortellini

They are called *sorpresine* [little surprises], and they are *tortellini* without the filling. They are made like normal *tortellini*: the pastry is as thick and as big as for *tortellini* but they are not filled and they are closed differently. This is also why they are called "empty *tortellini* upside down". *Sorpresine* are perfect for soups.

Tortellacci

Very large *tortelloni*. The right serving is 3 per dish, possibly of different colors: a red one, a green one and a traditional yellow pastry one. To make them, cut the pastry into strips and then into 14 cm squares. Fill them with different fillings, according to the color, and cook in the grill dressing them with egg béchamel (see recipe on page 91).

They can also be filled with savoy, lettuce and spinach.

Key

The pastry bag
It's a fabric bag, typically used to decorate and mould sweets (cream puffs, *spumoni*, cakes, etc.).
"Xenophiles" prefer to call it in French, *sac à poche*.
It is very present in Bolognese traditional recipes, often used to fill fresh egg pasta with tasty fillings.
It allows, pressing the top part of the bag, to put creamy fillings evenly, both sweet and savory.
But it can be used in many other ways as well: if your kitchen lacks a funnel, you can easily replace it with a pastry bag!

Tortelloni

To make *tortelloni*, use a knife or a specific cutter for *tortelloni* to cut the pastry into 6 cm wide strips. Cut the strips into 6 cm squares and fill them with *ricotta*, potatoes, salmon, truffle, rocket, *radicchio* or with a sweet filling. Use your hands or a pastry bag to put a knob of filling in the centre of each square. Finally, close them in the shape of triangles pressing firmly to keep the filling from pouring out. Then wrap them around your forefinger and close the two ends.

The typical filling is with *ricotta* and, according to the traditional recipe, they should be dressed with a butter and tomato sauce, also known as "butter and gold" (see recipe on page 83).

↑ One tortellone and one tortellaccio.

Home-made bread

Making bread at home is easier than you think. The mix of flour, yeast and water takes little time, as creating bread shapes with your hands.

The most challenging part is surely the rising, not for the technical difficulties that can occur, but for the various kinds of yeast and flour needed and for all the appropriate fermentation and kneading processes.

We will try to explain all these things as simply as possible, bearing in mind the practical aim of this handbook.

We will particularly take into account two kinds of yeast that are necessary to make homemade bread. *Brewer's yeast* and *"mother" yeast*. The first can be found in the form of cubes in stores, the latter is homemade and can be stored in the fridge for several weeks: add a little amount to the dough every time you make bread.

Moreover, in some recipes, we will suggest using *chemical yeast,* that is the yeast sold in sachets (16 g each and is used for 1/2 kg flour).

Bread dough: type 1 or mix to make "mother" yeast ✻

Ingredients and quantities for 4 bread loaves (400 g each), or for 24-26 rolls:

1 kg flour (type 0)
400 g water
50 g brewer's yeast
1 dl milk
1 tablespoon olive oil
1 teaspoon honey
20 g salt

Boil 400 g water with 20 g of salt. Add 1 dl of cold milk and let it become warm.

Meanwhile, melt 50 g of brewer's yeast, mixing it thoroughly with a teaspoon of honey and with olive oil in a cup. As soon as the water, with milk, becomes warm, add it to this mix and then add to 1 kg of flour, starting kneading on the board.

Process the dough with a fork first and then knead with your hands, using the same technique illustrated for pastry. Dose water and flour gradually and add a dash of salt. Knead the dough, without pressing it hard, until it's smooth and dense.

Let it rise for about 1 hour (in summer it takes less), covering with cellophane. Then knead the dough again (not for long, this time): divide it into 4 pieces if you want to make 400 g loaves, or into 24-26 pieces if you want to make smaller rolls.

Define the final shape, making loaves or rolls. You can also make breadsticks if you like.

Finally, put the shaped dough on the baking pan, with greaseproof paper, and let rise for about another hour.

Put in the pre-heated oven at 200° and bake for about 40-50 minutes.

Bread dough: type 2 ✳

Ingredients and quantities for 4 bread loaves (400 g each), or for 24-26 rolls:

1 kg soft wheat flour (type 0)
100 g melted fat
50 g brewer's yeast
5 g sugar
1/2 l whey or water
1 small piece of "mother" or natural yeast
20 g salt

Take a small piece of "mother" yeast from the dough prepared according to the previous recipe and add the other ingredients.

The dough is prepared with 1 kg of soft wheat flour (type 0), 50 g of brewer's yeast, mixed with 100 g of melted fat and sugar and with the whey extracted from cheese (see recipe on page 144). Add "mother" yeast and salt. Mix carefully until the dough is elastic. Cover with cellophane and let it rest. It is im-

portant to keep it from air because the heat makes it rise faster.

Let it rise for about 1 hour; then make loaves or rolls, as you prefer. Put them on a baking pan with greaseproof paper and let them rest to rise for about another hour.

Bake at 200° for 30 minutes.

Bread shapes

Bread can be shaped in many different ways using the same kind of dough: the classical family loaf; rolls shaped like artichokes, cylinders or bows or creating new shapes using our creativity. The process is the same for any kind of bread.

After the first rising, split the dough into small pieces according to the shape you want to make (following the quantities indicated in the recipe on pages 28-29). Make the appropriate sticks of dough, as thick as needed for the shape you want to make. Flatten the dough with your palms to make a long oval dish of dough.

Now you can let your creativity work…

Barilino

Simply roll the dough. Put on a baking pan and let rise until it becomes twice as big as it was. Make a deep cut over the half of the roll and bake.

Carciofo

Lay the dough vertically. Make many cuts, one every 1 or 2 cm, starting from the right and stopping in the middle. Cut this way all the right side of the dough strip. Roll the dough, pressing on the uncut part, and "open the artichoke", laying it on its base. Let it rise on the baking pan and then bake.

Crocetta or nodino

Lay the dough in front of you. Turn the tip upwards, make a fold and start rolling, keeping the dough on the opposite side with your left hand. Roll the dough up to the middle and then stop. Do the same with the other half of the dough, holding the roll that you have already made with your left hand. Once the two cylinders "meet" in the middle, twist the right-handed side cylinder twice. Then lift the central knot. Press lightly on the base before baking.

Breadsticks

To make breadsticks, prepare very thin dough sticks, 1 cm thick at the most or even thinner if you prefer thin breadsticks. Use your fingers to adjust and level the sticks' thickness while laying them on the baking pan, appropriately separated. Let them rise until they become three times as big. Bake.

Loaf

Use your right hand to fold the tip of the dough; then roll it with your palm, pressing a little and making a loaf with the middle a little thicker than the ends. Put it on the baking pan and let it rise according to the recipe. When it's twice as big, cut the surface deep up to the centre of the loaf and then bake.

Saint Petronius' bread ✳

Ingredients and quantities for 2 Petronian loaves, 350 g each:

for the dough:
500 g flour
25 g brewer's yeast
1 tablespoon olive oil
25 g butter
1 tablespoon cream
10 g salt
warm water (not hot)

for the filling:
50 g parmesan cheese
80 g ham
butter flakes

Make a well with 500 g of sifted flour and put 10 g of salt, 25 g of butter, 1 tablespoon of cream and 1 tablespoon of olive oil in the centre. Melt 25 g of brewer's yeast with at least a cup of warm water, not hot, and add it to the rest of the mix.

Mix the dough quickly and make a solid ball. Press it down on its base, making a cross on its surface with a knife or a blade. Cover carefully with two towels and a cellophane sheet.

Let it rise for 1 hour. Knead the dough again and split into two parts. Put back to rest both parts, covering them again.

Knead with your hands one part and then the other. Roll it out and then make two round pieces. Do not use the rolling pin in this stage.

Enrich each "dish" with a sprinkling of parmesan cheese and with slices of ham, until you cover the whole surface. Then add some more grated parmesan cheese. Roll the filled "dish" and join the two ends making a single loop. Use a sharp knife to make deep cuts on the surface. Finally, scatter flakes of butter on it and plenty of grated parmesan cheese.

Bake at about 200°C for about 30 minutes.

From a hearty tradition

Saint Petronious' bread is called like this because it is traditionally prepared on the day of the patron saint of Bologna (4th October).
Families used to make this special, rich bread to celebrate their patron saint. Saint Petronius' bread was not served during meals but it was enjoyed with relatives and close friends, along with a glass of good wine.

Bolognese-style mixed fry, sweet and savory

Bolognese-style mixed fry is considered one of the poorest dishes in Bolognese recipes but it is also one of the most requested in restaurants because it is very tasty.

It is rarely listed in restaurants and most of the restaurants that make it, only make it to order. Why? The answer is simple: it is a long and elaborate dish, rich in sweet and savory ingredients and very difficult to make because of its cooking method, which requires using many pans on the cooker at the same time. Moreover, it has to be served immediately in order to appreciate the various fried pieces at their best, when they are still crunchy.

From meat to vegetables, to *mortadella*, potato croquettes and sage and mint leaves, fresh fruit and sweet semolina and fresh egg custard. These are the components of the popular Bolognese-style mixed fry, which follows the culinary history of our ancestors, when families where large and food was little, with not enough meat and vegetables for everybody. Thus, dicing meat, cutting vegetables julienne, enriching each bit with flour and batter or with breadcrumbs and then frying everything you can serve a wonderful dinner, even using small quantities of each ingredient.

It is difficult to indicate a specific recipe for Bolognese-style mixed fry, with quantities and ingredients according to the number of people. Meat, vegetables and fruit are chosen according to the personal taste and, therefore, each element is dosed accordingly. We will only give you the standard recipe for semolina and egg custard.

Meat ✳ ✳ ✳

For fried meat you can use turkey, pork, chicken, lamb as well as beef or veal, although they are not typically used. All meat is processed carefully and made into little balls or small pieces.

Meat should be boned before being cut into pieces. After spraying the meat with some lemon juice, season with salt and pepper and let it rest for about 1 hour. Then lay it on roll paper or on a towel to dry; quickly dip into flour, then in the beaten egg, after seasoning it with salt and pepper and then in the breadcrumbs. Fry in fat.

Lamb: lean meat must be boned firstly and then diced; spare ribs, on the other hand, must be left whole. As for turkey, chicken, veal and beef, it needs to be sprayed with some lemon juice, seasoned with salt and pepper and then rest. Thus coat the dice with flour, then with the beaten egg and breadcrumbs. Plunge them into fat.

Pork: the process depends on the type of pork you want to cook. Fillet must be sliced and then processed as described for lean meat, boned and diced. Lean meat, on the other hand, must be ground and worked in a meatball. For example, 1 kg of meat should be mixed with 100 g of ground *mortadella*, 3 eggs and 200 g of parmesan cheese. Process the mix and adjust with salt, pepper and nutmeg. Use your hands to make small meatballs, dip them quickly into the flour and then in the beaten egg. Then, having put the breadcrumbs on a sheet of greaseproof paper, roll them on it until they are completely coated. After coating them, several times, plunge them in fat or in boiling oil to make a tasty crust.

Potato croquettes: boil potatoes – for example 1 kg – and mash them with the potato masher. Add 50 g of butter, 2 eggs and a dash of salt, pepper and nutmeg. Use your hands to shape mashed potatoes into cylinders or balls. Coat them with flour, then with salted beaten egg and finally coat them with abundant breadcrumbs.

Mortadella: dice it and soak it in cold milk for half an hour. Dry and then coat it, firstly with flour, then with the beaten egg and, finally, with breadcrumbs.

Vegetables ✻ ✻ ✻

Many kinds of vegetables can be used for the Bolognese-style mixed fry. It is advisable to chose vegetables in season.

Chop the vegetables in different shapes (according to the type of vegetable) and coat them with a batter to make them crispy.

It is important to plunge the vegetable bits in the fat when it gets to the smoking point, especially in the case of "battered" vegetables: this helps cook the dish in the right way and makes a perfectly crispy fry.

The batter is a mix of flour, sparkling cold water and a dash of salt: whisk until you get a creamy batter in which you will plunge the vegetables. When frying, the batter becomes immediately golden, making a thin crust: for this reason, the vegetables continue to cook inside, without getting mushy and keeping their water.

Potatoes: these are the only vegetables that don't need batter. Fry them before the others or they will take up the flavor of the other vegetables. Peel the potatoes and dice them. Transfer a pan with fat over heat and plunge the potato dice when it reaches the smoking point. They will immediately get colored on the surface, making a golden crust. Thus, the potato becomes immediately crispy outside and keeps on cooking inside without becoming soft.

Carrots: peel them and blanch them for 3 minutes in boiling water. Cool them and dry them. Cut them into slices and coat them with flour and batter.

String beans: string them and remove the two ends. Wash them and blanch them for about 3 minutes in salted water. Cool them. Coat them with flour and batter.

Celery: cut across according to the desired length and then vertically into strips, only using the soft part (as for *pinzimonio*) and discarding the outer stick. Then, wash with cold water and coat with flour and then with batter. Plunge them into boiling fat. Celery should stay crispy inside but not raw.

Artichokes: only use the heart. Cut it into 6-8 slices, which must be plunged into salted water, pre-

viously acidulated with lemon. Then, coat them with flour and batter. There is no need to blanch.

Zucchini: slice them according to the desired length. Cover them with salt for at least 20 minutes. Rinse thoroughly with cold water and then dry. Coat with flour and then with the batter.

Eggplant: dice into 1,5 cm cubes and plunge in salted water for half an hour. Rinse and dry carefully. Coat with flour and then with the batter.

Asparaguses: use only the soft part, as for artichokes. Blanch them for 3 minutes. Dry them, cool them and then chop them evenly. Coat them with flour and batter.

Broccoli: trim the broccoli into tiny florets. Blanch for 3 minutes, after chopping them into evenly-sized pieces. Dry them carefully and cool them. Coat them with flour and batter.

Cauliflower: as for broccoli, extract most of the heart and remove the tops one by one. Cut them into evenly-sized pieces and blanch them for 3 minutes. Dry them and cool them. Coat with flour and batter.

Zucchini flowers: wash them. Dry them laying them on a towel or using a salad spinner. Coat them with batter, without coating them with flour. Plunge them into boiling fat, making sure you remove them as soon as the coating becomes crispy.

Sage, mint and basil leaves: wash them in cold water. Dry them and coat them with flour and batter. Plunge them into boiling fat for just a few seconds. Remove them as soon as the batter becomes crispy, otherwise they would release water.

Violets: only use the violet flower, picked in a field or in the wood. Keep 1 cm of stem to dip the flower into the batter and then just a few seconds in fat.

Onions: slice them and open them. Wash them in acidulated water (mixed with 2 or 3 drops of vinegar) to help mitigate their strong odor. Coat them with flour and then dip them into the batter. Cook them at the end, in order not to give the fat their strong taste.

Tomatoes: they are very watery, so they should be cooked after all the other vegetables because they lower the fat's temperature. Dice and clean them without peeling them, just removing the seeds. Season with salt. Coat them with flour and then with batter and, finally, cook them for just a few seconds in boiling fat.

Don't forget...

The secret for crispy vegetables
Vegetables should be dipped in the batter right before plunging them in boiling fat.
For this reason, the batter should be made as you fry the bits.

Sweets

The sweet part of this varied dish consists of fried custard, semolina fritters and "fried" fruit.

Fried custard ✳ ✳ ✳

Ingredients and quantities for 6 people:

60 g flour
3 eggs
125 g sugar
1/2 l milk
a lemon peel
1 dash of salt
breadcrumbs as needed
icing sugar as needed
fat for cooking

Boil milk with the lemon peel. Meanwhile, mix 125 g of sugar, 3 eggs, 60 g of flour and 1 dash of salt in a bowl.

Add the flavored, hot milk and blend. Strain and put back on the heat.

Stir and keep cooking until it achieves the right consistency. It's the same recipe as for custard (see recipe on page 150).

When it is ready, lay it on a baking pan and level until you get an even sheet, about 1,5 cm high. Let it rest to cool.

Then, cut it into squares or sticks and coat with

breadcrumbs firstly, then with salted beaten egg and back with breadcrumbs (like a Wiener schnitzel!)

Plunge into boiling fat and remove as soon as they become crispy. Lay on roll paper and put it on the serving dish, dusting with icing sugar.

Semolina fritters ✳ ✳ ✳

Ingredients and quantities for 6 people:

1/2 l milk
60 g semolina
125 g sugar
raisins soaked in rum as desired
a grated lemon peel
1 dash salt
breadcrumbs as needed
1 egg
icing sugar as needed
fat for cooking

Blend 1/2 l of milk, 60 g of semolina, 125 g of sugar, 1 dash of salt and a grated lemon peel in a bowl. Add the desired quantity of raisins soaked in rum. Mix until you get a creamy compound and transfer to heat, still stirring.

When it is ready, lay it on a baking pan and level until you get an even sheet, about 1,5 cm high. Cut it into squares or sticks, as described for fried custard. Coat with breadcrumbs firstly, then with salted beaten egg and back with breadcrumbs.

Fry and dry on the roll paper. Serve on dishes after sprinkling the fritters with icing sugar.

Fried fruit ✳ ✳ ✳

Ingredients and quantities for 4 people:

250 g flour
500 g fruit at pleasure (apples, cherries, pears)
1 egg
1 tablespoon sugar
1 teaspoon maraschino or sambuca or anisette or brandy
milk as needed
1 dash of salt
fat for cooking

Preparation of the sweet batter for frying: after mixing flour and sugar, blend with cold milk until you get a dense batter. Add a yolk, setting the white aside, and keep stirring. Let it to rest in a fresh place for about half an hour, covering it with a sheet of cellophane. Whisk egg white until frothy with 1 dash of salt and add it to the other part of the batter.

Spray, as desired, with *maraschino* or *sambuca*, or with anisette or brandy, according to the kind of fruit to coat with batter.

Apples, for example, go well with *sambuca*, anisette and brandy, while cherries are better with *maraschino*. Pears, on the other hand, can be flavored with anisette.

Dip the fruit pieces in flour and then into the sweet batter. Fry them in boiling fat, turning them on both sides to make completely golden. Drain, dry them on roll paper and serve them hot.

Don't forget...

Suggestions for kitchen operators
Bolognese-style mixed fry is not a dish for beginners at all! We will try to give you some useful advice to manage its preparation. Start with the sweets, preparing the creams (even the night before) and letting them cool. Then bread the meat, following the above-mentioned recipe, and the fried custard and semolina fritters as well.
Vegetables and fruit, on the other hand, should be prepared and cook on the spot.
Remove any pot from the cooker and keep the space for at least 3 pots: one for meat, one for vegetables and one for sweets and fruit.

Polenta

Polenta is a very poor dish but is often dressed with tasty and rich sauces. Going back to the peasant origins of this dish, the traditional dressing is cheeses or *saracca*, also known as herring. However, today *polenta* is a dish that goes perfectly well with the tastiest and finest meat sauce.

Classic polenta *

Ingredients and quantities for 6-8 people:
700 g coarse cornmeal
300 g fine cornmeal
6 l water
salt as needed

There are mainly two ingredients for *polenta*: coarse and fine cornmeal, in the right amount. For example, for 1 kg of cornmeal, consisting of 700 g coarse and 300 g fine, put 6 l salted water to boil. When it's boiling, add coarse flour slowly and stir. Let it boil again and then turn the heat low, but enough to let it simmer. Let it cook for 40-45 minutes more, stirring every now and then to keep the *polenta* from sticking to the bottom of the pan.

It gradually becomes dense and creamy. At this point add fine flour with the help of a sieve. Keep it on the heat for 15 minutes more, stirring continuously, and then turn off.

Pour it on the wooden board, allow it at least 30 minutes to become compact and then slice it.

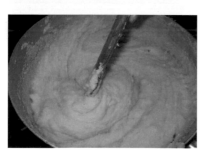

Don't forget...

The density of polenta
The traditional Bolognese *polenta* is quite dense but not as that from the Northern regions of Trentino or Valle D'Aosta.
If you prefer it to be less dense, simply add some raw butter when it's ready.
Liquid *polenta* is poured directly in dishes, ready to serve.

Fried polenta *

Once *polenta* is ready, cut it into 1,5 cm thick slices. Cook in boiling fat, letting them fry until the surface is colored. Fired bits of *polenta* are perfect as appetizers, served crispy and accompanied by appropriate dipping.

Toasted polenta with cheeses ✻

> **Ingredients:**
>
> sliced ready polenta
>
> **at pleasure:**
> soft cheese, stracchino, squacquerone, gorgonzola, taleggio and fontina

Cook *polenta* slices on the hot plate, toasting one side first and then the other. Serve on dishes along with soft cheese, *stracchino* or *squacquerone*. According to personal taste, there are also those who like it accompanied by *gorgonzola*, *taleggio* and *fontina*.

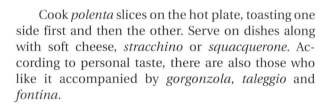

Polenta with sausage sauce ✻

> **Ingredients for 6 people:**
>
> **for polenta:**
> 700 g coarse cornmeal
> 300 g fine cornmeal
> 6 l water
> salt as needed
>
> **for sausage sauce:**
> 800 g sausage
> 1 onion
> 40 g stick of celery
> 40 g carrot
> 1 tablespoon fat
> white wine as needed
> 1 tablespoon tomato paste

Melt the fat in a pan. Dice the onion, 40 g of celery and 40 g of carrot and put stir fry for a few minutes. Cut part of the sausage into 3 cm thick pieces.

↑ Sliced polenta.

Mince the remaining part with a knife or with a meat mincer.

As soon as the vegetables are browned enough, add the minced sausage and let it cook on a high flame. After a while, the meat will turn its color to white; at that point, spray with wine and allow to evaporate. Finally add 1 tablespoon of tomato paste, melted with water. When it starts boiling again, add the sausage bits. Let it boil for 40-45 minutes more.

Prepare *polenta* as previously described (page 41): use the *polenta* left to cool down on the board and sliced.

Serve adding parmesan cheese at pleasure.

Polenta with pheasant ✻ ✻ ✻

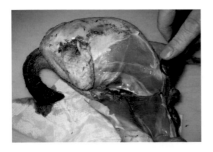

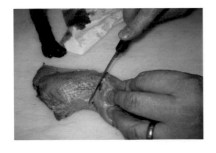

↑→   Pheasant cut.

Ingredients and quantities for 4 people:

1 kg pheasant
1 stick of celery
1 carrot
1 small onion
1 laurel leaf
1 tablespoon brandy
1 tablespoon red wine
some juniper berries
pepper as needed
nutmeg as needed

for polenta:
700 g coarse cornmeal
300 g fine cornmeal
6 l water
salt as needed

for the base for sauce:
flour as needed
a spray of brandy
fat for cooking

for the sauce:
1 average onion
1 tablespoon fat
some drops of olive oil
1 stick of celery

1 carrot
2 laurel leaves
3 garlic cloves
1 cinnamon tip
2 cloves
red wine as needed
flour as needed
salt as needed
pepper as needed

Cut the tip of the wings and the legs, the head and a part of the neck of the pheasant. Singe it on the flame to remove any small feather left; wash it with cold water and cut it into pieces (the breast should stay attached to the wing and the leg to the hip), setting the carcass aside. Marinate the breast and leg boned meat with 1 stick of celery, 1 carrot, 1 small onion, 1 laurel leaf and some juniper berries. Adjust pepper and nutmeg (no salt) and add 1 tablespoon of brandy and 1 of red wine, spraying them on the meat. Thus, the pheasant meat takes up the perfume of the other ingredients.

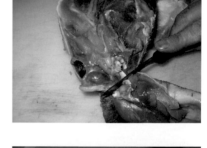

To prepare the base for the sauce: put some fat in a pot, put the carcass and the bones in pieces to prepare the base for the sauce. Let them fry, sprinkle with flour as soon as the bones get colored and spray with brandy. Cover with water and allow to boil for 3-4, even 5 hours, in order to make a thick cream consisting of the real taste of the pheasant.

How to prepare the sauce: the day after, put fat and some drops of olive oil in a pan. Dry the marinated pheasant bits, season with a dash of salt, adjust pepper and coat with flour. Add a coarsely chopped mix of 1 medium-sized onion, 1 stick of celery, 1 carrot, 2 laurel leaves and 3 garlic cloves to the fat. Mix with a cinnamon tip and 2 cloves, not chopped.

Allow to brown and finally plunge the pieces of meat coated with flour. Spray with a little red wine, allow to evaporate and gradually add the liquid (sifted) obtained from the carcass and bones, keeping the meat covered so that it simmers and stays tender.

Keep cooking for 20 minutes more and add water if necessary. Try it and adjust salt and pepper.

This tasty dish should be served with *polenta*, prepared according to the classic recipe (page 41).

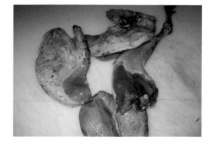

Polenta with pork spare ribs *

Ingredients and quantities for 4 people:

1 kg spare ribs
1 tablespoon fat
white wine as needed
6-8 garlic cloves
1 stick of rosemary (about 15 cm)
1 tablespoon tomato paste
salt as needed
pepper as needed

for polenta:
700 g coarse cornmeal
300 g fine cornmeal
6 l water
salt as needed

Sauté the spare ribs, previously seasoned with salt and pepper, with 1 tablespoon of fat. Spray with white wine as soon as the spare ribs start browning, making a crispy and golden film around them. Add 6-8 garlic cloves, the leaves of a stick of rosemary (about 15 cm) and 1 tablespoon of tomato paste, diluted with stock. Allow to boil again. Lower the heat and cook on a low flame for 1 hour and a half. Adjust salt and pepper.

It should be served with *polenta,* prepared according to the classic recipe (page 41).

Polenta with duck * * *

Ingredients and quantities for 4 people:

1 kg duck
flour as needed
salt as needed
pepper as needed

for polenta:
700 g coarse cornmeal

300 g fine cornmeal
6 l water
salt as needed

for the base of the sauce:
1 tablespoon flour
a spray of brandy
water as needed

for the sauce:
1 onion
1 carrot
2 garlic cloves
abundant brandy

Follow the same technique described for cleaning and cutting the pheasant. The night before cooking, prepare the base of the sauce with the bones, adding as much flour as needed to coat the carcass. Add a spray of brandy, cover with water and allow to boil for 3-4, even 5 hours, on a low flame in order to make a thick cream. Bone the meat; no need to marinate.

The day after, season the meat bits with salt and pepper and then coat them lightly with flour. Chop 1 onion, 1 carrot and 2 garlic cloves coarsely and put in a pan with 1 tablespoon of fat. Sauté the mix, browning only the outer part of the vegetables. Plunge the meat coated with flour, allowing to cook on a high flame. Spray with abundant brandy, flaming it.

Then, add the sieved base made with bones and allow to cook for 20-25 minutes more on a medium flame. Add more water if necessary. Finally, adjust salt and pepper.

It should be served with *polenta,* prepared according to the classic recipe (page 41).

Polenta with rabbit or chicken cacciatore ✳ ✳

Ingredients and quantities for 6 people:

1,5 kg rabbit or chicken
flour as needed
white wine as needed

for polenta:
700 g coarse cornmeal

↑↓   Chicken cacciatore cut.

300 g fine cornmeal
6 l water
salt as needed

for the sauce:
1 tablespoon fat
2 onions
1 tablespoon tomato paste
2 garlic cloves
1 handful rosemary
white wine as needed
stock or water as needed

Chicken and rabbit *cacciatore* are made according to the same recipe described for pheasant and duck.

Singe and wash the chicken, then cut it into pieces according to its joints. Remove its head and legs and set them aside to prepare stock (see recipe on page 105).

As for rabbit, remove its head and use it, along with the other pieces, to flavor the sauce; then cut it into pieces according to its joints. Wash the pieces with white wine. Dry them with care and coat with flour. Prepare a base of fat in the pan and add meat. Sauté on a high flame and spray with white wine. Slice 2 onions to sprinkle on the meat pieces. Season with 1 tablespoon of tomato paste, diluted with stock or water and allow to boil again. Add 2 garlic cloves and a pinch of rosemary. Keep cooking for 40-50 minutes, adding a little water every now and then to keep the meat tender.

It should be served with *polenta*, prepared according to the classic recipe (page 41).

Polenta with hare ✳ ✳ ✳

Ingredients and quantities for 6 people:

1 kg hare
red wine as needed
1 onion
1 stick of celery
1 carrot
3 garlic cloves
2 laurel leaves
2-3 crushed juniper berries

rosemary and laurel
lemon peel
flour as needed

for polenta:
700 g coarse cornmeal
300 g fine cornmeal
6 l water
salt as needed

for the base of the sauce:
flour
1 tablespoon fat
brandy as needed

for the sauce:
1 tablespoon fat
1 stick of celery
1 carrot
1 onion
2-3 garlic cloves
red or white wine
1/2 tablespoon tomato paste
salt as needed
pepper as needed

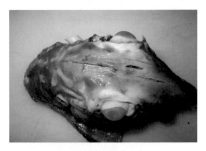

Cut the hare into pieces. Set the ribs, the head and the neck aside. Chop the selected meat into smaller pieces. Soak into red wine with 1 onion, 1 stick of celery, 1 carrot, 3 garlic cloves, 2 laurel leaves and 2-3 crushed juniper berries. Add sweet marjoram and thyme or basil. In winter, you can replace them with rosemary and laurel. What's important is that you always use fresh herbs, never dry spices.

Put the lemon peel on top. Cover with plastic wrap and store in the fridge all night.

Prepare the base of the sauce with the bones (head, neck and ribs). Put the fat in a pan, add the bones and sauté them. Add flour and spray with brandy. Allow to boil for at least 4 hours, covering with water. Prepare the sauce in a deep pan. Sauté 1 stick of celery, 1 carrot, 1 onion, 2-3 garlic cloves, all finely diced, into fat. As soon as they start to brown, add the meat chops, previously coated with flour. Spray with red or white wine, add 1/2 tablespoon of tomato paste, which helps soften the hare's strong taste, and stir with care. Add the base, sieved. Allow to cook for 30-40 minutes. Add more water in case it becomes too dry. Adjust salt and pepper.

It should be served with *polenta,* prepared according to the classic recipe (page 41).

↑ Rabbit cacciatore cut.

47

Polenta with guinea-hen ✳ ✳

Ingredients and quantities for 6 people:

1,5 kg guinea-hen
4 garlic cloves
1 stick of rosemary
salt as needed
pepper as needed

for polenta:
700 g coarse cornmeal
300 g fine cornmeal
6 l water
salt as needed

for the sauce:
1 tablespoon fat
2 onions
2 garlic cloves
200 g bacon
stock or water as needed

The typical product of the Park

Raviggiolo

A rare and soft dairy product with a delicate taste, which is a perfect match for *polenta*. It goes very well with fresh fruit jams as well.

Over the last centuries, *raviggiolo* was considered a delicious dish that could not be missed in banquets. It was mainly made with goat milk; today is mainly made with cow milk.

Its preparation does not involve breaking the rennet: just drain the block and add salt on the surface. It has a round shape, 2-4 cm high and cannot be stored for more than 4-5 days.

It is usually served on fern branches. It is produced from October to March.

Guinea-hen can be cooked in the same way as rabbit or chicken *cacciatore* (see recipe on page 45) or in the following alternative way, which includes bacon.

Chop the guinea-hen into quarters firstly and then into eighths, after singeing and washing it. Put the chops in a bowl and season with salt and pepper, 4 garlic cloves and 1 stick of rosemary.

Prepare the base in a wide pan with the fat, 2 julienned onions and 2 garlic cloves. As soon as the onion is browned, add 2 tablespoons of water and cover with a lid, in order to cook it without burning it. Turn off the heat when ready.

Sauté 200 g of bacon and add it to the browned onion. Turn on heat again. Add the meat to the julienned onions and the bacon; turn it on both sides. Then add 1/2 glass of water and allow to evaporate. Keep cooking, adding stock or salted water.

It should be served with *polenta,* prepared according to the classic recipe (page 41).

Polenta with dried salt cod ✳

Ingredients and quantities for 4 people:

1 kg dried salt cod
flour as needed
1 tablespoon seed oil
4 garlic cloves
3 tablespoons chopped parsley
1 tablespoon tomato paste
salt as needed
pepper as needed
3 drops of lemon juice

for polenta:
700 g coarse cornmeal
300 g fine cornmeal
6 l water
salt as needed

First of all, buy some good dried salt cod, white (not yellow) and fleshy. Soak it for 2 days to soften it, changing the water often.

Skin it completely and chop it into 5 cm cubes. Dry the chops and coat them with flour. Sauté them into seed oil and cook them thoroughly on each side.

Separately chop 4 garlic cloves and 3 tablespoons of parsley. Sauté in seed oil and then add tomato paste, diluted with water. Adjust salt and pepper. Allow to cook and add the dried salt cod sautéed chops as soon as it starts boiling. Allow to boil for 20 minutes more. The sauce should not be too dense nor too watery, but it must be creamy.

Final touch: before turning off the heat, add 3 drops of lemon juice and then turn off. Adjust salt and pepper according to personal taste.

It should be served with *polenta*, prepared according to the classic recipe (page 41).

The typical product of the Park

Pork cheek

This is a kind of cold meat obtained by the pork cheek, worked in patches of about 1 kg, in the shape of a triangle or trapezoid. Its thickness is never higher than 10 cm. The cheek is very tasty, mainly fat with some well-located lean parts.

Basically, the production stages are as follows: firstly, the pork cheeks are processed and, after trimming, are lain on boards where they are seasoned with a mixture of salt, garlic and pepper. The seasoning process lasts for about 2 weeks.

Then, each piece is brushed or washed and dried, and finally put to hang. Then, they are left to mature in a dry place for at least a month. Considering the high level of calories, we suggest eating it during winter.

It is a perfect starter, with home-made bread, or can be paired to fried *polenta* for a tasty meal. In some Italian regions, such as Latium, it is the main ingredient in sauces like *amatriciana* or *carbonara*.

Starters, appetisers and snacks

In this section of the book you will find the recipes to make tasty between-meal snacks that will also prove perfect for a buffet or a picnic lunch in the country. You may of course serve them as starters and some even as main courses.

We will discuss typical dishes such as fried *crescentine* (better known as *gnocco* in some parts of the Emilia area), *tigelle*, *piadine*, stuffed *crescente*, and rolled omelettes sided by tasty mousses and served with typical local products – choice cheese or sausages and pickled vegetables. Moreover, you will find plenty of quiches as well as soft, delicious flans.

Tuna butter ✳

Quantities:

500 g butter
250 g tuna
2 anchovies in olive oil
1 tablespoon capers
lemon juice
salt as needed
pepper as needed

Whip 500 g of butter and season with salt and pepper. In a blender, mince and mix 1 tablespoon of capers, 2 anchovies and 250 g of tuna.

Add the tuna mixture to the whipped butter; adjust salt and pepper and finally add some tablespoons of lemon juice.

Don't forget...

How to use flavored butter
If you have flavored your butter with tuna, baby artichokes, truffles or mixed pickled vegetables, use it to creatively garnish omelettes (e.g. a rolled omelette) or soften croutons and canapés.

Pickled vegetable or baby artichoke butter ✳

> **Quantities:**
>
> 500 g butter
> 500 g baby artichokes in olive oil, or mixed pickled vegetables or any leftover sauce
> salt and pepper as needed

Whip 500 g of butter; add the same quantity of minced baby artichokes (or mixed pickled vegetables or some leftover boiled meat sauce) and blend. Adjust salt and pepper.

Truffle butter ✳

> **Quantities:**
>
> 500 g butter
> truffles to taste
> a sprinkle of brandy
> salt as needed
> pepper as needed

Whip 500 g of butter, sprinkle with some truffle and mix. Season with salt, pepper, and a sprinkle of brandy.

Pickled baby onions ✳

> **Quantities:**
>
> fresh white baby onions
> red and white vinegar
> seed oil with olive oil (1 teaspoon per jar)
> salt as needed

Carefully peel onions; wash and soak them in red vinegar for at least 10 days. Drain and rinse with an abundance of white vinegar. Pack onions in glass jars, gently pressing them as not to leave any space. Cover with seed oil and add 1 tablespoon of olive oil. Let stand in a cool place.

Allow your pickled onions to stand for at least a

> **Remember that...**
>
> **Vegetables and fruit to be transformed and preserved**
> The vegetables you want to be preserved in oil or in pickle or to be transformed into preserve, like fruit, to be treated in alcohol or even to be processed marmalade-style, must be necessarily the ones in season. So, spring onions, artichokes in oil and etc. must be treated fresh, in the harvest time, thus following the phases belonging to the seasonal nature of the products, which vary from region to region.

> **Don't forget...**
>
> **How to clean onions**
> Onions of every size are cleaned by peeling outer leaves and trimming sprouts.
> Discard their roots, but set aside leaves (*la sgarbaza* in Bolognese dialect) to make a tasty omelette.

month before serving: they will prove a delicious side dish and an ideal all-year-round starter.

Stuffed crescenta with ciccioli or onion *

Ingredients and quantities for 15 servings:

700 g bread dough
70-100 g Parma ham or bacon ciccioli (fried scraps of pork meat), or 70-100 g onions

This dish was once called *la crescenta con i ranzett*, the latter being thin strips of ham or bacon. After kneading bread dough following the recipe on p. 28, add 70-100 g of ham or bacon *ciccioli* (or onions). Lay dough in a casserole lined with parchment paper. Bake at 180° for 40 minutes.

Cut your stuffed *crescenta* in the desired shape and serve.

Fried crescentine * *

Ingredients and quantities for 6-8 people:

1 kg flour
50 g brewer's yeast
35 g coarse salt
2,5 l water
1 dl milk
1,5 dl cream
1 teaspoon of honey
1 tablespoon of fat

Bring to a boil 2,5 dl of water with 35 g of coarse salt. Add 1 dl of milk and 1,5 dl of cream and stir slowly to bind ingredients together.

When liquid gets hot, start kneading 1 kg of flour with 50 g of brewer's yeast previously diluted in 1 teaspoon of honey melted in lukewarm water.

Knead dough with your hands, let stand and rise for about 30-40 minutes.

If you want to form your *crescentine* in circular shapes, divide dough into 6 small balls; alternatively divide dough in parts, and with a rolling pin roll it into squares or diamonds. Let rise for further 30 minutes, then roll again until 2-3 mm thick.

Fry the *crescentine* into boiling fat. When they swell and brown, remove them from heat and let dry in roll paper. Serve warm.

Erbazzone ✳ ✳

Ingredients and quantities for 6 people (in a 30 cm wide tin flan):

for the dough:
300 g flour
70 g fat
cold water as needed
salt as needed

for the filling:
1 kg mixed vegetables
1 tablespoon minced lard
50 g grated parmesan cheese
4 eggs
chopped parsley as needed
salt as needed
pepper as needed
nutmeg as needed

From a hearty tradition

On Easter Monday, commonly known as *Pasquetta* in Italy, people would go for a trip to the countryside or to the neighbouring hills near San Luca to have the traditional outdoor picnic lunch. Food was prepared beforehand, at home, and people would generally bring along the *crescenta* stuffed with *grasôl* or onions, and fried *crescentine* to be stuffed with sliced sausage, ham, soft or *stracchino* cheese right before serving.

Mix carefully 300 g of flour, 70 g of fat, a dash of salt with cold water as needed. Line a mould or a tin flan with dough, setting some aside you will later use as a lid. *Erbazzone* is usually stuffed with mixed vegetables (spinach, Swiss chard, chicory etc.): boil and chop the vegetables, then stir-fry with 1 tablespoon of minced lard in a preheated pan.

Rather than turning your vegetables with a fork or any other kitchen tool, shake them vigorously to lend flavour. Use abundant salt and pepper to season. Set aside.

Put 4 eggs, nutmeg, 1 tablespoon of minced parsley in a bowl; add some grated parmesan cheese (at least 50 g). Adjust salt and pepper.

Pour the filling into the mould or tin flan; cover

Don't forget...

It's better to serve your Erbazzone cold
It will gain flavor and taste much better. It's better to prepare it in the morning and leave it standing until dinner in order to allow flavors to bind together.

with dough, gently piercing on top. Bake at 160°-180° for 40-45 minutes.

Rolled omelette ✳ ✳

Ingredients and quantities for 6 people:

30 g flour
60 g butter
6 eggs
salt and pepper as needed

for the filling:
see recipes on pp. 50, 62 e 91

In a bowl, beat 6 eggs and adjust salt and pepper. Mix 30 g of flour with the beaten eggs.

Melt 60 g of butter in a pan and add it to the mixture in the bowl. Mix well to bind ingredients together, then transfer again to the frying pan. Cover and cook at medium-low heat, turning over the omelette once. Remove from heat and transfer to a serving plate; let cool.

Stuff your omelette with a savoury mousse – tuna mousse, *mortadella* mousse, cheese mousse – or some flavored butter – tuna butter, or butter flavored with baby artichokes or truffles – (see recipes from p. 62 to p. 91). Transfer the omelette to a serving dish, spreading its top with some mousse or flavored butter; roll omelette and serve sliced at will.

Don't forget...

Buffet omelette
When preparing a special meal or a buffet dinner, you may want to present your rolled omelette in several ways. Serve cut in round servings arranged on a tray and garnished with some mousse; alternatively, use it as filling for your canapés, making sure your rolled omelette is not wider than 5 cm.

Galantine or rifreddo ✳ ✳ ✳

Ingredients and quantities for 6-8 people:

30 g Parma ham
70 g mortadella

1 chicken weighing about 1,2 kg
650 g of pork (breast, not loin)
1 egg
salt as needed
pepper as needed

for the second layer:
2 boiled eggs
1 carrot
some black truffle flakes

for the aspic:
2 egg whites
salt as needed
pepper as needed.

for the gelatine:
1 celery
1 carrot
1 onion
1/2 glass of white wine
2 couple of veal
salt and pepper as needed

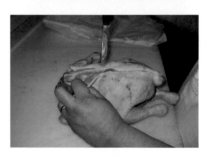

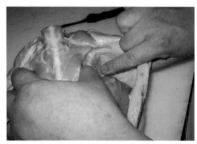

Starting from its back, bone chicken being careful not to tear the skin. Set skin aside to use later. Leave breast whole and cut it into fillets; set remaining thighs, wings and back aside.

Chop and mix *mortadella*, ham, and pork (or any other type of leftover meat) together; process through a mincer three or four times, or until getting a creamy mixture. Add egg and season with salt and pepper.

At this stage, lay chicken skin on the table. Arrange one layer of the mixture on the skin, then a layer of chicken breast fillets, then one of carrots (previously boiled and chopped), then one of sliced boiled eggs; sprinkle with some truffle flakes and top with a final layer of the mixture. Alternatively, replace truffle with black olives.

Carry on until you'll have two layers of each kind. Seal the chicken skin around the "meatloaf"; roll it up carefully in a tea cloth before boiling in the stock.

In the meantime make the stock for the aspic. In a large, deep stock pan, arrange the chicken carcass and then the herbs (celery, carrot and onion). Add 1/2 glass of white wine and season with salt and pepper. Cover with water, bring to a boil and cook for 50-60 minutes. Turn off heat and let cool. Strain cooking liquid through a fine sieve; add a couple of veal or

↑ Chicken cut for galantine.

55

beef or pork knee bones and bring again to a boil. Simmer for 4 or 5 hours.

Let cool and strain again; beat 2 egg whites and bind them carefully to the stock; bring to the boil and let simmer for about 1 hour.

When foam thickens and stock gets clearer, aspic has formed. Drain it gently through a sieve, adjusting salt and pepper.

Your meatloaf will have become firm by then. Remove from cloth, slice thinly and serve topped by the aspic.

The galantine or *rifreddo* is a major typical dish in the Bolognese tradition. Nowadays it is served as a tasty appetiser.

Mixed pickled vegetables ✳ ✳

Ingredients:

celery
carrots
onions
baby artichokes

for the pan:
some extra celery, carrots and onions
2 l water
0,5 l white vinegar

for the jars:
50% seed oil + 50% olive oil
salt as needed

for pan of the baby artichokes:
1 l oil (50% olive oil, 50% seed oil)
1/2 glass white vinegar
1 whole lemon juice
coarse salt and pepper as needed

Fill a pan with 2 l of water; turn heat on, adding 0,5 l of white vinegar and salt as needed.

Wash celery, carrots and onions: trim celery into big sticks, chop carrots (discarding hard parts), cut onions in halves (or leave whole if small).

When water starts boiling, plunge celery sticks and cook for 4 minutes; remove and leave to dry. In the same cooking liquid, plunge onions and cook for 5 minutes; remove and leave to dry. Finally plunge carrots and boil for further 5 minutes.

Do not boil thoroughly boil your vegetables, but cook them slightly so as to keep them crispy on the inside.

Let vegetables cool, then transfer to the jars. At your will, mix or leave vegetables separated, covering one half with seed oil and the remaining half with olive oil.

Keep cool. Let stand until the next morning, but it is better to have them stand for at least a month.

If you choose to make pickled baby artichokes, you should remember these require a different cooking and keeping process.

Pour 1 l of oil (half olive, half seed oil). Add 1/2 glass of white vinegar and the juice of a whole lemon. Season with coarse salt pepper. In the meantime, trim baby artichokes, keeping tender parts only. Chop and leave soaked in liquid.

Transfer the pan over high heat; bring it to the boil, then cook for further 3 minutes. Turn off heat and let cool. Fill jars with baby artichokes and their liquid. Keep cool.

Allow your pickled baby artichokes to stand for at least a month before serving.

Piadina ✻

Ingredients and quantities for 6-8 people:
1 kg flour 20 g fine salt 2 chemical yeast sachets 2 full fresh liquid cream tablespoons 0,5 l milk

Mix and knead 1 kg of flour, 30 g of chemical yeast, 0,5 l of milk, 30 g of salt and 2 abundant tablespoons of fresh cream. Handle gently till dough gets

Curiosity

Piadina recipes transcend tradition

Everybody knows *piadina* comes from the coast area of Romagna. The following recipe is an easier version, which doesn't aspire to be the best and original one. As a matter of fact, among its ingredients you will not find fat, a constant feature in the traditional dough.

This is an ever-ready dish! Dough keeps well in the fridge, allowing you to prepare a meal based on *piadine and crescentine* for your friends in a handful of minutes.

firm. Leave standing for at least 1 hour, then divide it in smaller parts. Using rolling pin roll dough out until about 3 mm thick.

Cook the *piadina* in special cast iron discs or iron pan. Roast shortly, turning occasionally to do both sides and prick with a fork, to let air to escape.

↓→ Puff pastry preparation.

Quiche Lorraine ✳ ✳

Ingredients and quantities for 6 people (for a 30 cm wide tin flan):

for the puff pastry:
500 g flour
500 g butter flakes
1,2 dl di acqua fredda
20 g salt

for the filling:
500 g onion
150 g smoked bacon
150 g cooked ham
80 g parmesan cheese
4 whole eggs
200 g fresh cream
1 oil tablespoon
1 knob of butter
rice or dry legumes

Make the puff pastry first: try to always knead more than 500 g of puff pastry, the minimum quantity required for the Quiche Lorraine, to keep the remaining part in the freezer.

For 1 kg of puff pastry, mix and knead 250 g of flour with 500 g of butter flakes; form into a rectangular shape and set aside. Mix and knead 250 g of flour with 250 g of cold water and 20 g of salt; roll into a rectangular shape until as thick as half your little finger. Place the flour and butter mixture onto the dough and spread it on top using your hands or a rolling pin. Fold pastry in two, to cover the flour and butter slab; roll again to incorporate. Fold dough it in three, forming a square, then refrigerate for 1/2 hour. Remove from fridge and repeat folding process at least twice, each time rolling, folding and refrigerating.

Start making the filling in the meantime. Cook 500 g of finely sliced onions in oil and butter without browning.

Let cool and add 150 g of smoked bacon, 150 g of cooked ham, 80 g of parmesan cheese, 3 eggs, 200 g of fresh liquid cream.

Line a tin flan with the puff pastry, arranging some rice or dry legumes that will keep pastry well pressed while baking.

Cook in the oven at 160° for 30 minutes. Remove the rice or legumes and pour mixture over puff pastry. Bake for further 20 minutes.

Sfilzini ✳

Ingredients and quantities for 6 people:

200 g mortadella
200 g diced cheese (edamer or emmenthal)
2 eggs
2 tablespoons milk
thin sticks (similar to toothpicks)
breadcrumbs as needed
salt as needed
pepper as needed
milk as needed
flour as needed

Cut *mortadella* and cheese into equal dice; pierce through the sticks following this order: 1 *mortadella* die, then a cheese die, and again a *mortadella* one. Soak in milk for 5 minutes.

In the meantime, mix eggs, salt and pepper in a bowl. Remove your *sfilzini* from milk: first dredge in flour, then in beaten eggs seasoned with salt and pepper, and finally in breadcrumbs. Plunge into boiling fat for a few seconds.

Serve your *sfilzini* warm as a snack or with an aperitif. You may as well add them to the Bolognese style mixed fry (see recipe on p. 33).

White flan with giblet meat sauce ✳✳

Ingredients and quantities for 6 people:

for the flan:
150 g butter
50 g parmesan cheese
4 eggs
salt as needed
pepper as needed
nutmeg as needed

for the béchamel:
2,5 dl milk
25 g butter
15 g flour
salt as needed
nutmeg as needed

giblet meat sauce:
500 g beef
150-200 g of gizzards, hearts, livers, ovaries
100 g celery
100 g carrots
100 g onions
1 tablespoon fat
red wine as needed
tomato paste as needed

Make a white flan and set aside. Prepare some béchamel sauce (see recipe on p. 90); stir in 150 g of butter, 4 eggs, 50 g of grated parmesan cheese, salt and pepper; mix well and pour mixture in a mould previously buttered and sprinkled with flour and breadcrumbs. Cook in bain-marie in the oven at 160° for about 50 minutes. Set aside. To make the giblet meat sauce, brown the chopped vegetables – 100 g of celery, 100 g of carrots, 100 g of onions – in 1 tablespoon of fat. Add 500 g of minced beef and cook over high heat. Spray generously with red wine. Let evaporate and add the tomato paste diluted in stock. Bring to the boil, then reduce heat.

After about 1 hour add the previously diced chicken gizzards. Cook for further 40 minutes, then add the finely chopped hearts. Finally add livers and hen ovaries.

Cook for 10 minutes. Transfer the white flan to a serving dish, top with the giblet meat sauce and serve.

Meat or fish flan ✳ ✳

Ingredients and quantities for 6 people:

400 g pureed fish or meat
150 g butter
1 tablespoon minced onion
4 eggs
40 g grated emmenthal cheese
salt as needed
pepper as needed
nutmeg as needed

for the béchamel:
2,5 dl of milk
25 g butter
15 g flour
salt as needed
nutmeg as needed

Don't forget...

The king of leftovers
Meat or fish flan is considered to be the king of leftovers!
Recycle all boiled, roasts, or *cacciatore* meat leftovers: the latter will give your flan an especially delicious flavour.

Brown 1 tablespoon of minced onion with 40 g of butter. Add 400 g of pureed meat or fish (a soft mixture made from leftovers), and season with salt, pepper and nutmeg. Stir in béchamel (see recipe on p. 90), along with 40 g of grated emmenthal. Mix ingredients with 4 egg yolks.

In the meantime, whisk egg whites until frothy and add to mixture; stir very gently to bind ingredients.

Pour into a buttered mould and cook in bain-marie in the oven at 160°. When flan top gets crisp, remove from the oven and let cool.

Vegetable flan ✳ ✳

Ingredients and quantities for 6 people:

for the flan:
700 g pureed vegetables
150 g butter
40 g parmesan cheese
4 eggs
salt as needed
pepper as needed

Don't forget...

Tips for a successful vegetable flan
Stuff your flan with just one type of pureed vegetables, or with several layers of different vegetables.
For a better baking, use a long, narrow mould (as the one used for the creme caramel), or a holed mould. Make your flan a couple of days beforehand, keep in the fridge and bake when needed.

nutmeg as needed

for the béchamel:
2,5 dl of milk
25 g butter
15 g of flour
salt as needed
nutmeg as needed

Start by pureeing vegetable, choosing at your will spinach, peas, asparagus, carrots, Swiss chard, chicory, herbs, and potatoes. After washing and draining vegetables, brown in a preheated frying pan along with 150 g of butter seasoned with salt, pepper, and nutmeg. Let cook until water dries up completely.

In the meantime, prepare your béchamel sauce (see recipe on p. 90); add it to the vegetables, along with 4 eggs, 40 g of grated parmesan cheese, salt and pepper and mix well. Pour into an oven mould previously buttered and sprinkled with flour and breadcrumbs, then cook in a bain-marie in the oven at 160°. It will be done when flan top gets crisp.

Cheese mousse ✳ ✳

Ingredients and quantities for 6-8 people:

500 g mascarpone flavoured gorgonzola cheese
250 g butter
2 egg whites
salt as needed
pepper as needed

In a bowl, whip 250 g of butter; set aside. In another bowl, whip 2 egg whites until frothy. Stir in 500 g of *mascarpone* flavored *gorgonzola* cheese and adjust salt and pepper. Mix with whipped butter until getting a smooth, soft mousse.

Mortadella mousse ✳ ✳

Whip 2 egg whites until frothy and add a dash of salt.

Blend 250 g of butter until getting a soft mousse; adjust salt and pepper. Add egg whites, 500 g of minced (at least three times) *mortadella*, and 1 teaspoon of brandy to butter. Stir gently.

Refrigerate mousse for at least 2 hours before serving.

Don't forget...

Mousse shapes
When decorating your buffet table, form your mousse in the desired shape, or serve it in special trays, siding canapés and croutons.
Each guest will spread some mousse on his slice of bread.

Tuna mousse ✳ ✳

Whip 250 g of butter until frothy. In another bowl, whisk 150 g of tuna, 1 tablespoon of capers, 2 anchovies in olive oil and some lemon drops. Adjust salt and pepper. Add to whipped butter and stir gently until getting a smooth firm mixture.

Tigelle ✳ ✳

Ingredients and quantities for 6-8 people:

1 kg flour
50 g brewer's yeast
100 g fat
1,5 dl white wine
milk as needed
20 g salt

Mix carefully 1 kg of flour, 50 g of brewer's yeast, 100 g of fat, 20 g of salt, with 1,5 dl of white wine and enough milk to make the dough. Mix and knead until your dough gets softer than the one commonly used for puff pastry.

Once it gets smooth, divide it in balls according to the size of the moulds of your *tigelliera*. Preheat moulds and transfer the balls to the special spaces provided in the tool.

Cook your *tigelle* for 5 minutes, turning them once. Transfer to a bowl, cover with a tea cloth. Serve warm.

Your *tigelle* will keep well in the freezer. Reheat them in a frying pan or in the oven some minutes before serving.

Don't forget...

A delicious pesto sauce
We are not providing the quantities for a precise number of guests, as we advise you make your *pesto* also for keeping.
Mince 500 g of lard with 2 garlic cloves and some rosemary leaves. Season with salt and pepper and finally add some grated parmesan cheese.
You will get a tasty mixture especially suitable to stuff your *tigelle*: cut a *tigella* in two halves, stuff it, and heat it up to soften the filling.
This pesto will keep well if refrigerated and soaked in seed oil in glass jars.

Onion pie ✳ ✳

Ingredients and quantities for 6 people (in a 30 cm wide tin flan):

for short pastry:
300 g flour
140 g butter
1 dl water
1 dash of salt

for the filling:
400 g onion
3 eggs
2 dl fresh cream
parmesan cheese (at will)
salt as needed
white pepper

For the short pastry (to prepare night before):

make a well with the flour, add some butter cubes, 100 g of water and 10 g of salt. Mix well and wrap pastry into transparent film; refrigerate for about 1 hour. Roll pastry to about 3 mm thick.

Finely slice the onions; cook them in salted water for about fifteen minutes. Drain and allow cooling, then add to 3 beaten eggs along with 2 dl of cream. Season with salt and pepper.

Line a mould with the short pastry, pouring mixture over; bake in the preheated oven at 200° for 30 minutes.

Version 1: at your will, add other vegetables, using fewer onions.

Version 2: instead of short pastry, use pizza dough, which is the same as the bread one (see p. 28).

Savoury pie ✳ ✳

> **Ingredients and quantities for 6 people (in a 30 cm wide tin flan):**
>
> **for the short pastry:**
> 300 g flour
> 140 g butter
> 1 dl cold water
> 1 dash of salt
>
> **for the filling:**
> 150 g ricotta cheese or béchamel sauce
> 25 g parmesan cheese
> 3 eggs
> salt as needed
> pepper as needed
> nutmeg as needed

For the short pastry base, make a well with the flour, adding 140 g of butter flakes, 1 dash of salt and 1 dl of cold water. Mix and knead quickly; don't leave standing, you may use it right away.

Roll the pastry with a rolling pin on some parchment paper until it gets wide enough to be lined over tin flan.

Your savoury pie can be stuffed in various ways; the base is always the same: 150 g of ricotta cheese or béchamel sauce (see recipe on p. 90), 250 g of parmesan cheese, 3 eggs, salt, pepper and nutmeg.

At your will, add one or several kinds of vegetables, such as asparagus, artichokes, spinach, Swiss chard, chicory, *radicchio*, or rocket to the mixture. You may also use some radicchio sauce or some other vegetable sauce leftovers as stuffing.

Mix leftover sauce to the mixture and spread over the short crust pastry already lined in the tin flan. Bake at 160°-180°, making sure both top and bottom are done before turning heat off.

Zucchini pie ✱ ✱

Ingredients and quantities for 6 people (in a 30 cm wide tin flan):

500 g zucchini
200 g ricotta cheese
50 g parmesan cheese
6 eggs
100 g butter
1 tablespoon minced onion
1 garlic glove
1 tablespoon olive oil
minced parsley as needed
salt as needed
pepper as needed
nutmeg as needed

Discard edges from the zucchini and trim in round shapes about 3 mm thick. Set aside. Mix 200 g of ricotta cheese, 50 g of parmesan cheese and 6 eggs. Season with salt, pepper, nutmeg, and sprinkle with parsley. Cook in a frying pan with 1 tablespoon of minced onion, 1 garlic clove, 1 tablespoon of olive oil and 100 g of butter. Wash the zucchini and transfer to a frying pan without drying. Adjust salt and pepper. Cover and cook over medium-low heat, but don't let them brown too much. When they stop frying, remove lid and make cooking liquid dry up. Add to mixture and bake at 160°-180°.

As for the other flans, your pie will be done when its top gets crisp.

Don't forget...

Not only zucchini
A zucchini pie is an excellent starter, and tastes great even served cold.
You may replace zucchini with other vegetables, such as eggplants or buttered carrot leftovers.

Fresh pasta dishes

Fresh pasta dishes are the so-called traditional rich dishes: this fresh pasta, simple or filled, and enriched with the many sauces described below, consists of several ingredients and its preparation is laborious.

In this section, we will not neglect the typical *balanzoni* with butter and sage sauce or the *ricotta tortelloni* with their typical butter and gold sauce, although we will look more in depth at some modern kinds of filling, going beyond tradition to some inventive fillings that have somewhat "contaminated" the typical dishes, in order to meet modern needs.

These are fillings that go well with any kind of filled pasta: *tortelloni, ravioli, caramelle, cestini, triangoli, pollicioni* and *mezzelune*. Fillings that can be used with a touch of fantasy, some of them probably suggested by the moment's fashion.

Balanzoni with butter and sage sauce ✳ ✳ ✳

Ingredients and quantities for 6 people:

for green pastry:
300 g flour
2 medium-sized eggs
30 g boiled and strained spinach
nutmeg flavor

for the filling:
250 g *ricotta*
25 g boiler and strained spinach
30 g butter
a few leaves of fresh basil or 1 dash of dried basil
75 g ground mortadella
50 g grated parmesan cheese
1 egg
salt as needed
pepper as needed
nutmeg flavor

The typical product of the Park

Parmesan cheese
It's one of the main ingredients of Bolognese cooking. The manufacturing technique of this precious cheese, one of the most famous in the world, dates back to the 12th Century, to Benedictine and Cistercian Monks. Today, the technique is exactly the same: only after maturing for one year, but the average is about 18-24 months, this cheese is ready for assessment. If it passes the test, it is sold with its typical brand.
The strict laws and regulations related to its production ensure a high average quality of Parmesan cheese produced in the provinces of Parma, Reggio Emilia, Modena, Bologna and Mantova. However, the quality of cheese produced in the National Park of the Tosco-Emiliano Apennine is definitely higher, mainly on account of the way milk animals are fed, basically with mountain forage.
Moreover, a wonderful milk, richer in proteins and with a better yield, is the one produced by the *Reggiane* red cows: an ancient race, which originated Parmesan cheese but features only two thousand items today. Parmesan cheese made with this milk is as excellent as rare.

After preparing the green pastry, mixing 300 g of flour, 30 g of boiled and strained spinach, 2 medium sized eggs, nutmeg flavor, let the dough rest, covering it with a cellophane sheet. Prepare the filling, mixing 250 g of ricotta and 25 g of sautéed spinach with 30 g of butter in a bowl. Season with salt and pepper and add some leaves of fresh basil or 1 dash of dried basil. Add also 75 g of ground *mortadella*, 1 egg and 50 g of grated parmesan cheese. Adjust salt, adding nutmeg flavor.

Roll out a thick pastry and make *balanzoni* with the filling (see recipe on page 24).

Cook in boiling water and dress with butter and sage.

Cannelloni Gratin ✳ ✳

Ingredients and quantities for 6 people:

for yellow pastry:
3 eggs
300 g flour

for the filling:
1 egg
500 g ricotta
100 g parmesan cheese
150 g mortadella
200 g strained spinach
salt as needed
pepper as needed
nutmeg as needed

for the sauce:
200 g mortadella
a sprinkling of grated parmesan cheese

for the béchamel sauce:
0.5 l milk
45 g butter
30 g flour
salt as needed
nutmeg as needed

After kneading the mix of 3 eggs, roll out a thin pastry. It is possible to use both the yellow pastry and the green one, or mixed of both colors. Cut it into 10-12 cm squares. Prepare the filling with 1 egg, 500 g of ricotta, 100 g of parmesan cheese, 150 g of ground *mortadella* and 200 g of strained spinach, sautéed in butter with salt and pepper.

Cook the pastry squares in salted boiling water, dry and lay them on a slightly oily board. Fill the square with the mix and roll it gently, closing it without pressing it.

Put a thin layer of béchamel sauce on the baking pan (see recipe on page 90). Arrange the *cannelloni* on the pan and cover with the béchamel sauce. Spread 200 g of Bolognese sauce, trying to give an even color to the sauce. Finally, sprinkle with parmesan cheese. Brown in oven for about 15 minutes at 180°.

The ideal serving is 3 *cannelloni* for person.

It is advisable to arrange single servings to be served directly in small casseroles.

Bolognese sauce lasagne ✳ ✳ ✳

Ingredients and quantities for 6 people:
for the green pastry:
3 eggs
300 g flour
20 g spinach
nutmeg as needed
for the sauce:
150 g grated parmesan cheese
800 g bolognese meat sauce
for the béchamel:
1 l milk
90 g butter
60 g flour
salt as needed
nutmeg as needed

Knead a 3 egg pastry: 300 g of flour, 20 g of spinach and a dash of nutmeg: the pastry for *lasagna* should be rolled out quite thick. Cut pastry on the board according to the shape and size of the pan you are going to use.

Cook the green pastry in salted boiling water, remove it when "al dente" and put it in a bowl with salted cold water, just for a few seconds to stop it cooking. Meanwhile, prepare the sauce aside, keeping 1 l béchamel sauce (see recipe on page 90), 150 g grated parmesan cheese and 800 g of previously cooked Bolognese sauce (see recipe on page 94).

At this point, the recipe must proceed quickly. Take the pastry out of the water without drying it, in order that it stays wet. Spread the Bolognese sauce on the bottom of the pan (preferably the oiliest part). Arrange the pastry without pressing, pour the béchamel sauce on it and then the Bolognese sauce. Spread with care, covering the whole surface of the pastry. Enrich with a sprinkling of parmesan cheese. Fill at least five layers using the same process.

Bake the pan at 180° for about 40 minutes.

If *lasagne* have been stored in the fridge or in the freezer, it is advisable to thaw them in the oven, covered firstly and uncover them after 10 minutes.

Lasagne with artichokes ✳ ✳ ✳

Ingredients and quantities for 6 people:

for pastry:
400 g flour
4 eggs

for the sauce:
4 artichokes
1 small onion
1 garlic clove
1 teaspoon dried oregano
1/2 tablespoon olive oil
150 g butter
1/2 glass of white wine
1/2 tablespoon flour
salt as needed
pepper as needed
parmesan cheese and emmenthal at pleasure

Clean 4 artichokes and discard the hard tips. Soak them in cold water, previously acidulated with some drops of lemon juice. Keep the soft part only: the heart and the stalk, cleaned. Cut them into two parts vertically and then again into three pieces, until you get small chunks.

Prepare a base of 150 g of butter and 1/2 tablespoon of olive oil in a deep pan. Sauté 1 finely chopped onion with 1 chopped garlic clove. Allow the onion to brown and add the artichokes, cooking them until dry. Add 1/2 glass of white wine and allow to evaporate, but not completely. Adjust salt and pepper and, finally, add 1 teaspoon of dried oregano. Stir the artichokes, add 1/2 tablespoon of flour (using a big tablespoon) and stir with care so that the flour doesn't become lumpy. When "the fats" start frying again, it's time to add cold water. Allow to cook until it becomes creamy. At this point, add all the water, about 1 l.

Meanwhile, prepare a 4 egg pastry and roll it out. Cut it into squares according to the indications of the traditional recipe (see recipe on page 69) and boil the layers. Arrange them on the pan, starting with a layer of sauce and dressing abundantly. Sprinkle cheese with care: it is better not to use only parmesan cheese because it is not sweet enough. It is advisable to mix parmesan and *emmenthal* cheese.

Bake at 180° and brown. *Lasagne* are ready when they puff up.

Don't forget...

Lasagne with artichokes in small casseroles
If you have guests for dinner, arrange the *lasagne* in small casseroles, one per serving.
Your guests will appreciate the dish even more if decorated with stringy cheese.
An additional touch can be adding some truffle slivers and, at pleasure, a spray of brandy to the béchamel sauce.
Storage: all kind of *lasagne* can be stored in the freezer, except for those with angler and shrimps or with cheeses.

Red lasagne with cheeses ✳ ✳ ✳

Ingredients and quantities for 6 people:

for the red pastry:
300 g flour
2 big eggs
1 abundant tablespoon of tomato paste

for the sauce:
150 g gorgonzola cheese
80 g grated parmesan cheese

for the béchamel sauce:
1 l milk
90 g butter and 60 g flour
salt and nutmeg as needed
150 g diced cheeses: edamer, fontina and others according to taste

Knead 300 g of flour, 2 big eggs and 1 tablespoon of tomato paste and roll out the pastry. Cut it into squares according to the traditional *lasagne* recipe (see recipe on page 69).

Prepare the béchamel sauce (see recipe on page 90), add 150 g of gorgonzola cheese, 80 g of parmesan cheese and boil. Meanwhile, dice edamer, *fontina* and other cheeses, according to taste.

Boil the "sheets" of pastry according to the traditional technique. Grease a pan with butter and then arrange the first layer of pastry with abundant béchamel sauce (see recipe on page 90), with the diced cheeses on top.

Make up to 4 layers: this kind of *lasagna* should be short and wide. Complete the last layer only with pastry and some flakes of butter and parmesan cheese.

Bake at 180° in a pan.

Lasagne with angler and shrimps ✳ ✳ ✳

Ingredients and quantities for 6 people:

for the pastry:
300 g flour
3 eggs

for the sauce:
200 g angler
150 g shrimps
100 g edamer or sweet emmenthal cheese: grated or julienne
1 small garlic clove
1 tablespoon finely chopped onion
50 g butter
1/2 glass of white wine
a spray of brandy
salt as needed
pepper as needed
flour as needed

Prepare 3 egg pastry and roll it out very thin (as for *tortellini*). Clean 200 g of angler and 150 g of shrimps. The fish remains, along with the shells and heads of the shrimps, will be boiled in a pan, adding as much water as needed to cover them completely. Salt lightly and allow to cook for 20 minutes, then sift the liquid and set aside.

Prepare the sauce: melt 50 g of butter with 1 chopped garlic clove and 1 tablespoon of chopped onion. Sauté on a low flame, without browning and flame with 1 tablespoon of brandy. Spray with 1 glass of white wine. When three quarters of the wine have evaporated adjust salt and pepper and add the liquid obtained from boiling the shells and the remains of the angler. Allow to cook on a low heat for 15 minutes.

At this point, sprinkle with flour the angler and shrimp chops. When the liquid boils vigorously, add the fish and allow to cook for about 5-10 minutes.

Tip: if the fish is not very tasty, add a dash of tomato paste right after spraying with wine and before adding the liquid previously set aside.

Cook the pastry in boiling water, flavored with some shrimp shells. Only for this type of *lasagne*, it is advisable to dry the pastry after cooking because the filling is watery enough. Arrange no more than 5 layers.

Bake and sprinkle with edamer or sweet emmenthal cheese. Cook for 40-45 minutes at 180°. Allow to rest 10 minutes before serving.

Maccheroni and peas pie ✳✳

Ingredients and quantities for 6 people:

for the pasta:
250 g flour
100 g fat
1 egg
1 dash of salt

for the pie:
500 g maccheroncini

400 g meat sauce with peas
50 g of grated parmesan cheese

for the béchamel sauce:
0.5 l milk
45 g butter
30 g flour
salt as needed
nutmeg as needed

Firstly prepare pasta: mix 250 g of flour, 100 g of fat and 1 dash of salt. Blend and make a well with 1 egg in the middle. Mix adding a little cold water, if the dough tends to crumble. Put in the fridge to rest for 30 minutes, covered with a cellophane sheet.

Then, roll out the pastry and split it into two parts: a larger one to lay on the mould or on the pie dish; a smaller one to be used at the end as a "lid". Fill the base of the pie with 500 g of *maccheroncini*, cooked and dressed with 400 g of meat-sauce with peas. Finish adding 0.5 l of béchamel sauce (see recipe on page 90) and 50 g of grated parmesan cheese. Cover with the smaller piece of pastry and bake for 40-45 minutes at 180°.

Lettuce Ravioli ✳ ✳

Ingredients and quantities for 6 people:

for the pastry:
4 eggs
400 g flour

for the filling:
1.2 kg lettuce
100 g sausage
100 g cooked ham
150 g grana padano
2 yolks
salt as needed
pepper as needed
nutmeg as needed

for the asparagus cream:
50 g butter
6 asparaguses
milk as needed
1/2 glass of cream
salt as needed

pepper as needed
nutmeg as needed

Cook the lettuce in salted boiling water for 10 minutes. Make it lukewarm adding cold water and strain. Wrap it with a cloth and squeeze it carefully. Mince 100 g of sausage, 100 g of cooked ham and, finally, the lettuce. Add 150 g of *grana padano*, 2 yolks, salt and nutmeg and stir all the ingredients vigorously.

Meanwhile, knead a 4 egg pastry. Roll it out and lay the filling on it using a pasty bag or with your hands. Fold it, press with your hands along the borders and cut with the pastry cutter. Now prepare the asparaguses cream sauce.

In the meantime, put the water for cooking *ravioli* to boil, adding the tips of 6 asparaguses. Clean their stalks and sauté in a pan with 50 g of butter. Add the milk and allow to cook, adjusting salt, pepper and nutmeg. When ready, process them with a vegetable mill. Finally, add the cream to get a smooth cream.

Strain the *ravioli* together with the asparaguses tips, dress with the asparaguses cream and serve.

Red turnip ravioli ✳ ✳

Ingredients and quantities for 6 people:

for the pastry:
4 eggs
300 g flour

for the filling:
150 g chopped red turnip
50 g grated parmesan cheese
350 g *ricotta*
30 g ground almonds
1 yolk
salt as needed
pepper as needed

for the sauce:
100 g butter
1 large tablespoon of onion
2 glasses of white wine
2.5 dl stock
poppy seeds
3 juniper berries

Mix 150 g of chopped red turnip, 50 g of parmesan cheese, 350 g of *ricotta*, 1 yolk, 30 g of ground almonds, salt and pepper.

Roll out a 4 egg pastry and make *ravioli* (recipe on page 25).

Fill *ravioli* with the filling and prepare the sauce for dressing them. Brown the onion with a little butter and spray with 2 glasses of white wine.

Add the juniper berries and allow to cook until it shrinks to the half. Add 0.25 l of stock and boil for 2-3 minutes. Put the *ravioli* in the butter and lay the sauce and poppy seeds on them.

Potato and meat ravioli ✳ ✳

Ingredients and approximate quantities:
for the red pastry: eggs   flour
for the filling: leftover meat   boiled potatoes   parmesan cheese   eggs

When you have leftover meat and you don't know how to use it, you can help yourself with this recipe. The quantities and ingredients of the pastry and the filling vary according to the quantity of the meat we are going to use.

Process the leftovers with the meat-mincer twice and weight the resulting mince meat.

Put the same amount of boiled potatoes, after mashing them when still hot. Mix the meat and potatoes. Add eggs and parmesan cheese to the filling (200 g and 1 egg for every kg of mix). Adjust salt, pepper and nutmeg.

Weight the resulting mix and roll out the red pastry, using as many eggs as required for the filling. The right quantity for the pastry is 1 egg per 150 g of filling.

Make the *ravioli* and preferably dress with butter with parsley (see recipe on page 91).

Sole-fish ravioli ✳ ✳

> **Ingredients and quantities for 6 people:**
>
> **for pasta:**
> 300 g flour
> 4 eggs
>
> **for the filling:**
> 300 g clean sole
> 100 g Piedmontese ricotta
> 1 yolk
> 1 dash of anchovy paste

Mince 300 g of sole and add 100 g of Piedmontese *ricotta*, 1 yolk and a dash of anchovy paste. Blend with care.

Meanwhile, roll out a 4 egg pastry, according to the traditional recipe (see recipe on page 25). Prepare and fill the *ravioli* with the fish filling.

The sole-fish *ravioli* are very tasty and go very well with a simple sauce such as "butter and gold" or butter and parmesan cheese.

Spinach roll ✳

> **Ingredients and quantities for 6 people:**
>
> **for the pastry:**
> 300 g flour
> 3 eggs
>
> **for the filling:**
> 500 g ricotta
> 100 g chopped, strained, cooked spinach
> 50 g parmesan cheese
> 1 egg
> salt as needed
> pepper as needed
> nutmeg as needed

Don't forget...

Pasta roll with fancy fillings
You can enrich pasta and spinach rolls coating them with béchamel sauce or adding some diced cooked ham.
The pasta roll can also be filled with a sausage and chicken liver sauce or with a mushroom sauce. In order to do that, make the filling according to the traditional recipe but replace spinach with the desired ingredients.

Prepare a 3 egg pastry. Cut it into rectangles and cook in a wide pan with salted, boiling water. Allow to cool and lay on a moist board, as for *cannelloni*.

The filling should consist of 500 g of *ricotta*, 100 g of finely chopped, strained, cooked spinach, 50 g of

parmesan cheese, 1 egg, salt, pepper and nutmeg. Spread the filling with care on the whole surface of the pastry, roll and cut it into 3 cm thick rolls. Arrange them on a gratin dish previously greased with butter and finish them with some butter flakes and a sprinkling of parmesan cheese. Bake at 180°.

Tagliatelle Bolognese ✳ ✳

Ingredients and quantities for 6 people:
for pasta:
600 g flour
6 eggs
for the sauce:
60 g onion
25 g carrot
20 g celery
1 tablespoon of lard
300 g beef
2 tablespoons of tomato purée
salt as needed
pepper as needed

Don't forget...

Leftover tagliatelle
Leftover *tagliatelle* can become precious: dress with meat sauce or with ham and sauté in a pan. A little butter can help make them even crispier.
In the same way, if they are unseasoned, you can sauté them in a pan, adding only a little nutmeg.
A simple but tasty flavor.

Knead a 6 egg pastry and make *tagliatelle* (see recipe on page 22).

Prepare the meat sauce browning 60 g of onion, 25 g of carrot and 20 g of celery in 1 tablespoon of lard. Then, add 300 g of beef and 2 tablespoons of tomato purée. Adjust salt and pepper (see recipe on page 94).

Plunge *tagliatelle* in salted, boiling water and stir them rapidly with a wooden fork. Strain when they come to the surface of the water and put them in a bowl. Add the meat sauce along with some tablespoons of hot water to keep the right humidity.

Taglioline with salmon ✳ ✳

Ingredients and quantities for 4 people:

for pasta:
400 g flour
4 eggs

for the sauce:
1 teaspoon of chopped onion
50 g butter
5 tablespoons of white wine
1 tablespoon of cognac
1/2 tablespoon of framboise
1 dl fresh cream
100 g salmon
30 g parmesan cheese
30 g emmenthal cheese
salt as needed
pepper as needed

Prepare a 4 egg pastry, allow to rest, well wrapped in a cellophane sheet and then roll it out. Make *taglioline* (see recipe on page 22). Brown 50 g of butter and 1 teaspoon of chopped onion. Spray with 5 tablespoons of white wine. When it boils, add 1/2 tablespoon of cognac, of framboise, or any other raspberry liquor. Blend until creamy, add 1 dl of cream and 100 g of diced salmon. Adjust salt and pepper. When ready, add 30 g of parmesan cheese and 30 g of emmenthal cheese.

Put the *taglioline* in the pan with salmon and serve.

Three-color tortellacci ✳ ✳ ✳

Ingredients and quantities for 10 people (3 tortellacci per serving, each of a different color):

Green tortellacci

for the pastry:
250 g flour
2 eggs
20 g spinach

for the A filling:
130 g tortellini filling
30 g spinach with butter
70 g grated parmesan cheese
120 g mixed ricotta
1 yolk
salt as needed
pepper as needed

for the B filling:
170 g balanzoni filling
70 g grated parmesan cheese
130 g ricotta cheese
1 yolk
salt as needed
pepper as needed

Red tortellacci

for the pastry:
250 g flour
2 eggs
1/2 tablespoon tomato

for the filling:
70 g gorgonzola cheese
70 g parmesan cheese
200 g ricotta cheese
1 yolk
salt as needed
pepper as needed
nutmeg as needed

or
250 g ricotta romana
80 g mascarpone
200 g gorgonzola cheese
70 g grated grana padano
1 yolk
salt as needed
pepper as needed

Yellow tortellacci

for the pastry:
300 g flour
3 eggs

for the filling:
garlic oil (garlic flavored)
1 tablespoon parsley
70 g grated parmesan cheese
300 g ricotta
1 yolk
salt as needed
pepper as needed
nutmeg as needed

The dish consists of 3 *tortellacci*, all different in color and filling. It is advisable to prepare this disch for at least 10 persons.

The green *tortellaccio*, after kneading 2 eggs, 250 g of flour and 20 g of spinach, can be filled with a mix consisting of 130 g of *tortellini* filling (see recipe on page 67), 30 g of spinach with butter, 70 g of grated parmesan cheese, 120 g mixed *ricotta*, 1 yolk, salt and pepper.

A variant can be: 170 g of *balanzoni* filling, 70 g of grated parmesan cheese, 130 g of *ricotta*, 1 yolk, salt and pepper.

The red *tortellaccio*, replacing the spinach in the dough with 1 tablespoon of tomato paste, can be filled with cheeses: 70 g *gorgonzola*, 70 g of parmesan cheese, 200 g *ricotta*, 1 yolk, salt, pepper and nutmeg. An alternative filling can consist of 250 g of *ricotta romana*, 80 g of *mascarpone*, 200 g of *gorgonzola*, 70 g of grated *grana padano*, 1 yolk, salt and pepper.

The traditional pastry *tortellaccio*, consisting of 3 eggs and 300 g of flour, can be filled with *ricotta prezzemolata*, which includes 300 g of *ricotta*, 70 g of grated parmesan cheese, 1 yolk, a drop of garlic oil, 1 tablespoon of chopped fresh parsley, salt, pepper and nutmeg.

Serve the three-color *tortellacci* with butter and abundant parmesan cheese.

Garlic and parsley straccetti ✽ ✽

Ingredients and quantities for 6 people:

500 g flour
5 eggs
1 chopped garlic clove
2 tablespoons of chopped fresh parsley
pepper as needed

Knead 5 eggs, 500 g of flour, 1 chopped garlic clove, 2 tablespoons of chopped fresh parsley and a dash of pepper. Blend the mix and roll out the pastry thick; cut strips 3 or 4 cm wide. Cook in salted boiling water and take out when they come to the surface. The ideal dressing for this pasta is the clam or shrimp sauce, or a vegetable sauce (see recipe on page 102).

Salmon tortelli ✷ ✷ ✷

Ingredients and quantities for 4 people:

for the pastry:
220 g white flour
2 eggs
1 tablespoon olio
1 dash salt

for the filling:
200 g smoked salmon
100 g ricotta
50 g goat cheese
3 yolks
1 teaspoon of chopped parsley
salt as needed
pepper as needed

for the sauce:
50 g butter
20 g flour
30 g shallot
1 teaspoon chopped parsley
100 g julienned salmon

Mix 220 g of flour with 2 eggs, 1 tablespoon of oil and 1 dash of salt. Cover the dough and let it rest in a fresh place for 30 minutes.

Mince 200 g of smoked salmon, then add 100 g of *ricotta* and 50 g of goat cheese. Add 3 yolks and 1 teaspoon of parsley. Adjust salt and blend.

Roll out the pastry and finish the *tortelloni*. Fill the pasta.

Make béchamel sauce with 30 g of butter, 20 g of flour and milk (see recipe on page 90) and adjust salt. Brown the chopped shallot in 20 g of butter, add 100 g julienned salmon and 1 tablespoon of parsley. Cook the *tortelli* and then dress them with the béchamel and the salmon sauce.

Ricotta tortelloni ✳ ✳

Ingredients and quantities for 6 people:

for the pastry:
3 eggs
300 g of flour

for the filling:
500 g ricotta cheese
70 g grated parmesan cheese
1/2 egg
20 g chopped parsley
salt as needed
nutmeg as needed

Roll out a 3 egg pastry to make *tortelloni* (see recipe on page 27).

Mix 500 g of *ricotta* cheese, 70 g of grated parmesan cheese, 1/2 egg and 20 g of chopped parsley in a bowl. Adjust salt and nutmeg.

Use this mix to fill the *tortelloni*, to dress with "butter and gold" preferably (see recipe on page 92).

This filling can be used for other kinds of filled pasta as well.

Truffled tortelloni ✳ ✳

Ingredients and quantities for 6 people:

for the pastry:
4 eggs
400 g flour

for the filling:
150 g lean chicken
150 g veal
100 g Parma ham (lean)
2 eggs
truffle flakes as needed
butter and cheese for seasoning
salt as needed
pepper as needed

Mince 150 g of lean chicken, 150 g of veal and 100 g of Parma ham, after removing its fat. Blend the mince meat with 2 eggs and the truffle flakes. Season

↑ *Tortelloni* cooking.

83

The typical product of the Park

The violina pumpkin
The land of the Regional Park of *Delta del Po* is perfect for growing pumpkins: an orange-fleshed and sweetish vegetable, which characterizes the filling of the traditional *cappellacci* (from Ferrara) or *tortelloni* (from Bologna).
The story goes that this ancient ingredient was already enjoyed by the noble members of the House of Este and that once, after the flesh was removed, it was used to carry water or wine and to store gunpowder.

From a hearty tradition

The "dirty soup" or "dirty pasta"
The Lent lunch is celebrated on Good Friday. The traditional lunch, strictly without meat, includes *ricotta tortelloni* with butter and gold or *gnocchi*, followed by a dish of eggs and spinach. The Bolognese tradition doesn't include fish.
In the past, people used to have a soup instead of *tortelloni*, which was called "dirty soup" or "dirty pasta": it consisted of peas soup with a very special kind of pasta. The pasta was prepared rolling out the pastry on the board and spreading a cheese cream on it (parmesan cheese, *stracchino* and nutmeg) or the *tortelloni* filling, enriched with the cheese cream; the other half of the pastry was used to cover it and then the pastry cutter was used to cut squares or rectangles to be cooked in the peas soup.

with salt and pepper. Roll out a 4 egg pastry and make *tortelloni* (see recipe on page 27), filling them with this mix.

Cook the *tortelloni* and season them with melted butter and abundant grated parmesan cheese.

Pumpkin Tortelloni ✳ ✳

Ingredients and quantities for 6 people:

for the pastry:
4 eggs
400 g flour

for the filling:
1 kg of pumpkin (500 g of cooked pumpkin)
50 g of macaroons
100 g parmesan cheese
1 yolk
salt as needed
pepper as needed
nutmeg as needed

Prepare a 4 egg pastry and make *tortelloni* (see recipe on page 27).

Cook 1 kg of pumpkin (or use 500 g of cooked pumpkin) for 30-40 minutes in the oven at 200°. Once you turn off the oven, leave the pumpkin inside for about ten minutes. Remove the outer crust and extract the pulp. Squeeze it wrapping it in a palm.

Then blend 50 g of macaroons, 100 g of parmesan cheese and 1 yolk with care. Add salt, pepper and nutmeg. Finally fill the *tortelloni* with this mix.

Season with butter and parmesan cheese or with the ham sauce (see recipe on page 98).

Fillings for all kinds of filled pasta

Rocket filling

Ingredients and quantities for 6 people:

70 g rocket
170 g grated *pecorino*
700 g *ricotta romana*
1 egg
1 spray of Worcester sauce
1 teaspoon olive oil
1/2 garlic clove
salt as needed
abundant pepper

Crush 1/2 garlic clove with 1 dash of salt, until you mash it with the help of a knife. Add it to the chopped rocket and blend with 170 g of *pecorino* cheese, 700 g of *ricotta romana*, 1 egg, a spray of Worcester sauce, 1 teaspoon of olive oil and abundant pepper. Adjust salt and fill the pasta.

Preferably season with butter and tomato, or parsley-flavored butter or olive oil and pepper.

Walnut filling

Ingredients and quantities for 6 people:

300 g ricotta cheese
60 g ground walnuts
100 g parmesan cheese
1 egg
salt as needed
nutmeg as needed

Mix 300 g of *ricotta* cheese, 60 g of ground walnuts, 100 g of parmesan cheese, 1 egg, salt and nutmeg with care. Blend thoroughly until you have a smooth mix and fill the pasta (made adding 10 g of black olive paté to the traditional pastry ingredients per 100 g of flour and per egg). Pasta with this filling can go very well with a vegetable sauce, for example with zucchini and eggplant, or with a spinach velouté.

It can also be served with butter and parmesan cheese.

Potato filling

Ingredients and quantities for 6 people:

500 g potatoes
100 g parmesan cheese
2 eggs
1 tablespoon of parsley
salt as needed
pepper as needed

Blend 500 g of boiled and mashed potatoes with 100 g of parmesan cheese, 2 eggs, 1 tablespoon of parsley. Adjust salt and pepper and fill the desired pasta.

Preferably season with spicy sauces: garlic, olive oil and pepper or butter and *provola* cheese or even tomato and chili pepper.

Radicchio filling

Ingredients and quantities for 6 people:

100 g grated parmesan cheese
500 g ricotta cheese
250 g radicchio
1 egg
salt as needed
pepper as needed

Cook 250 g of *radicchio* on the grill, in the oven or in a pan without any oil. Chop it and add it to 500 g of *ricotta* cheese, 1 egg, 100 g of grated parmesan cheese, salt and pepper. Blend the ingredients and fill the pasta.

Season with butter with parsley or with olive oil, pepper and a sprinkling of walnuts or pine nuts.

Vegetable filling

Ingredients and quantities for 6 people:

200 g zucchini
200 g eggplant
300 g ricotta romana
100 g robiola cheese
30 g grated grana padano
1 yolk
salt as needed
pepper as needed

Clean the vegetables: 200 g of zucchini and 200 g of eggplants without peeling them. Finely dice them and allow to rest in separate bowls with salted cold water for half an hour.

Them fry them in separate pans with olive oil and dry with roll paper.

Blend the vegetables with 300 g of *ricotta* cheese, 100 g of *robiola* cheese, 30 g of grated *grana padano*, 1 yolk, salt and pepper.

Fill the desired pasta and season with tomato, garlic and basil or olive oil and pepper.

Savoy filling

Ingredients and quantities for 4 people:

500 g savoy
40 g lard
40 g butter
50 g grated parmesan cheese
25 g breadcrumbs
1 onion
1 stick of celery
1 tablespoon of parsley
salt and pepper as needed
nutmeg as needed

Clean 500 g of savoy, removing the central stick and plunge it into salted boiling water. Cook for 10 minutes after it starts boiling again. Strain and let drip dry.

Finally chop 40 g of lard and melt it in 40 g of butter. Finally chop 1 onion, 1 stick of celery, 1 tablespoon of parsley as well and add to the lard.

Brown the mix on a low heat, add the savoy leaves and allow to cook for about 20 minutes, in a half-covered pan, in order to make it completely dry.

Finely chop the remaining ingredients and put them in a bowl.

Add 50 g of grated parmesan cheese, 25 g of breadcrumbs, salt, pepper, nutmeg and blend with care. Fill the desired pasta and season with melted butter and parmesan cheese or with "butter and gold".

Sweet filling

Ingredients and quantities for 6 people:

80 g crumbled bitter macaroons
50 g raisins
40 g dry cookies
80 g grana padano
35 g citron
1 whole egg
1 tablespoon alchermes
20 g dark chocolate
a grated lemon peel
salt as needed

Knead the pastry with 250 g of flour, 1 egg, 1 yolk, 1 knob of butter, 1 small tablespoon of oil, 1 dash of salt and a little warm water. Allow to rest at least half an hour before rolling it out.

Meanwhile, blend 80 g of macaroons, 50 g of raisins, 40 g of dry cookies, 80 g of *grana padano*, 35 g of citron, 1 whole egg, the grated peel of 1 lemon, 20 g of dark chocolate, 1 tablespoon of alchermes and 1 dash of salt.

Mix the ingredients in a blender and fill the desired pasta.

Season with strong sauces that are in contrast with the sweet taste of the filling. The simplest is:

oil, pepper and grated *pecorino*. Avoid sweetish sauces such as sauces based on tomato.

Table: Proportion between the number of eggs and the quantity of fresh pasta to make per person. ↓

Eggs Quantity	Pasta weight	Filling quantity	Persons
5 eggs	Simple pasta: tagliatelle, strichetti, garganelli etc. 750 g		5-6 people
5 eggs	1,5 kg of tortelloni	750 g of ricotta	10 people
5 eggs	1,5 kg of tortellini	750 g of filling	15 people
5 eggs	2 cannelloni baking-tins for 6	1,5 kg of filling	10 people
5 eggs	2 lasagne baking-tins for 6		12 people
5 eggs	2 spinach rolls baking-tins for 6	1,3/1,5 kg of filling	10 people
5 eggs	2 kg ravioli	1,3 kg of filling	15 people
5 eggs	1,6 kg pollicioni	1 kg of filling	10-12 people

↓ A sfoglina's tools.

Sauces and seasonings

Who doesn't know the delicious Bolognese sauce? It has "traveled" so much, both in Italy and abroad, that it has suffered many variations – often unacceptable ones – that have upset the historic-gastronomic value of the original recipe.

However, while sticking to the tradition, this chapter illustrates the typical Bolognese meat-sauce and its complex preparation as well as other famous sauces (sausage meat-sauce, ham and peas meat-sauce, giblets meat-sauce and many others). You will also be illustrated some very simple sauces, such as "butter and gold" and the butter and cinnamon, which can perfectly match all pasta dishes.

Moreover, we will also go beyond the tradition, describing some sauce, certainly faster and more modern ones, that have gained their place in our houses over the last decades. For example, the sauce with shrimps and zucchini, the salmon or *gorgonzola* sauce as well as a very light vegetable sauce.

Béchamel sauce *

Ingredients and quantities for 1 l of milk:
1 l milk 90 g butter 60 g flour salt as needed nutmeg as needed

Warm 1 l of milk with 1 dash of salt and nutmeg. Melt 90 g of butter, adding 60 g of flour, in a separate pan. Stir gently and, as soon as the flour foams, pour the mix in the boiling milk.

In the Bolognese tradition, béchamel sauce is used for baked pasta, *lasagne*, *cannelloni* and other filled kinds of pasta.

Béchamel sauce with eggs *

> **Quantity per 700 g:**
>
> 4 dl milk
> 2 dl cream
> 20 g flour
> 100 g butter
> 2 yolks
> salt as needed
> nutmeg as needed

Melt 100 g of butter in a pan and add 20 g of flour, stirring gently.

Add 4 dl of boiling milk with 2 dl of cream.

Season with 1 dash of salt and a sprinkling of nutmeg. Lead to boil, while stirring, and then turn off heat. Finally, add 2 yolks. Pass through a sieve.

Egg béchamel enriches first courses and side dishes browned in the oven: potato *gnocchi*, cannelloni and spinach *rondella* rolls, or even thistles, cauliflowers, broccoli and fennels.

Flavored butter seasoning

> **Ingredients and quantities for a pat:**
>
> 200 g of butter
> fresh herbs as desired (marjoram, thyme, mint, sage, parsley, rosemary)

The flavored butter is to be prepared without heating.

Put the 200 g of butter (not from the fridge) in a bowl. Add the fresh herbs you desire, such as marjoram, thyme, mint, parsley, sage, rosemary, or a chopped mix of all these. There are no specific quantities related to the quantity of butter, they depend on personal taste.

Flavored butter is a perfect sauce seasoning for any kinds of pasta.

Butter and cinnamon seasoning ✳

> **Ingredients and quantities for a pat:**
>
> 200 g of butter
> 1/2 cinnamon stick

Opposite to the herbs used for flavored butter (see the previous recipe), cinnamon needs to be dosed correctly, according to the quantity of butter. A small quantity is enough to flavor the butter.

Mix 200 g of butter with 1/2 cinnamon stick (about 1 cm) until smooth.

The butter and cinnamon seasoning goes particularly well with potato *gnocchi*.

Butter and gold sauce ✳

> **Ingredients and quantities for 6 people:**
>
> 500 g of peeled tomatoes
> 200 g of butter
> salt as needed

Put 500 g of peeled tomatoes (or tomato purée) in a pan without heating. Blend 200 g of butter and allow to cook for 10-15 minutes. Remove from heating and use a hand-held mixer to beat the sauce until creamy.

Traditionally, this sauce matches perfectly with *gnocchi* and *tortelloni*.

Cheese and basil sauce ✳

> **Ingredients and quantities for 6 people:**
>
> 150 g of mascarpone cheese
> 100 g finely diced cheeses (pecorino, emmenthal, others)
> 1 tablespoon of gorgonzola cheese
> some chopped fresh leaves of basil

salt as needed
pepper as needed

The main ingredients of the cheese and basil sauce are basically two: the *mascarpone* cheese, which has the seasoning function, and *gorgonzola* cheese, which makes it tastier. Make a creamy sauce with 150 g of *mascarpone* cheese and 100 g of finely diced mixed cheeses (*gorgonzola*, *pecorino*, emmenthal). Adjust salt and pepper.

Strain the pasta and, when still moist, put it into the bowl where the cheese cream has been previously mixed: the cream will melt with the heat of the pasta. Add some cooking water if necessary. Adjust salt and pepper, if needed. Finally, decorate with a sprinkling of fresh basil.

The cheese and basil sauce goes very well with garlic and parsley *straccetti* as well as with simple pasta, such as *strozzapreti* and *ricotta gnocchi*, or even with *maccheroni* and large *rigatoni*.

Zucchini and shrimp sauce ✳

> **Ingredients and quantities for 6-8 people:**
>
> 12-15 shelled shrimps
> 500 g of zucchini
> 1 tablespoon of chopped onion
> 1 garlic clove
> salt as needed
> 2 tablespoons of oil
> white wine as needed
>
> **another version:**
> 1 dash of anchovy
> 1 teaspoon of tomato

Dice 500 g of zucchini and soak in salted cold water for about half an hour.

Make the base for the sauce, browning 1 tablespoon of chopped onion and 1 garlic clove. When brown, add the zucchini removing them from the water. Cover with a lid for just a few minutes and then cook without lid; stir every now an then, making sure the zucchini do not overcook. Finally add 12-15 shelled shrimps and allow the tastes to blend for 5 minutes.

> **Don't forget...**
>
> **Pots and pans: do's and don'ts**
> Earthenware and aluminum pans are perfect, even better if kept separate according to their use: a pan for stock, one for Bolognese sauce, another for other sauces and one more for soups.
> Definitely avoid non-sticking and stainless steel pans: the first can really change the color of food, while the latter cannot be used for tasty cooking, as they absorb flavors.
> A definite yes for iron and enamel pans, which are good for frying.
> The same rule applies to frying pans: iron, aluminum and tin-plated copper are fine. Avoid stainless steel ones.

The zucchini and shrimp sauce can be used to season *gnocchi*, *strichetti* or *straccetti*.

It is also possible to make a variant of this dish: the *sorpresine* (see recipe on page 26) with zucchini and shrimp sauce. In this case, don't let the sauce dry but add a little water when cooked, after adding the pasta to the sauce. When they are ready, eat using a tablespoon.

Sausage mix ✳

Ingredients and quantities (for 1,5-2 kg mix):
1 kg of pork stewing steak (shoulder) 700 g of fresh bacon 1 chopped garlic clove 1 dl of white wine 50 g of salt as needed 8 g of pepper

If you want to make sausages at home, you need to mince 1 kg of pork stewing steak (shoulder) and 700 g of fresh bacon. Add the seasoning: 50 g of salt, 8 g of pepper, 1 chopped garlic clove and 1 dl of white wine. Blend the mix and put into the specific pork bowels to make sausages.

Sausages can be stored in the fridge or freezer for a long time. It can also be left 10 days out to dry, thus making a dry sausage.

The same mix can be used to make meatballs or to make sausage meat-sauce.

↓ Bolognese meat-sauce preparation.

Bolognese meat-sauce ✳ ✳

Ingredients and quantities for 8 people:
150 g of onion 70 g of carrots 50 g of celery 50 g of lard

600 g of beef (neck or shin)
1 or 2 glasses of red wine
1 bottle of tomato purée or tomato paste
salt as needed
pepper as needed

Wash and peel 150 g of onions (removing the inner sprout in order not to modify the final taste of the sauce (see box on page 51) 70 g of carrots, 50 g of celery, only using the stalks and discarding the leaves.

Put 50 g of lard on the heat and add the seasoning vegetables, after mincing them into a single mix. Once, the grounding and crushing of the seasoning vegetables was made with *la pistadura*, consisting of a special knife and the board.

Brown the vegetables on a medium heat. The base is ready when the vegetables change their color and are completely dry. They will gradually turn to a light hazel color. The rule *La conza las fa cold nes* applies, that is "Bolognese meat-sauce must be prepared according to the way it smells…": it is ready when you cannot smell the carrot, celery and onion separately, but a single perfume.

At this point, it is necessary to lower the heat and allow the base to stew. Brown the vegetables until they are well cooked, though not boiled.

Spread with care the base so that it covers evenly the bottom of the pan (also aluminum pans are used today, whereas only earthenware pans were used in the past).

Mince 600 g of beef (neck or shin). Do not use the back parts of the animal for this sauce, as they are suitable for steaks.

Add the mince meat to the vegetables and brown on a high heat. Add salt and pepper and stir with care. The meat will gradually become the same color of the vegetables. Add 1 or 2 glasses of red wine and keep stirring.

Blend the mix carefully until you cannot smell the meat separately from the wine. At this point add about 1 bottle of tomato purée or tomato paste.

Lower the heat and allow to boil slowly, stirring every now and then, for more than 2 hours, adding a little stock or water if necessary.

Don't forget...

How to store the meat-sauce

If you want to store the meat-sauce, it is necessary to set it aside before adding tomato, interrupting its cooking. This meat-sauce, the so-called white one, can be stored in the freezer. When you need it, remove from the freezer and continue to cook it as described before. It will take 2 hours. The cooking can be completed in the traditional Bolognese way or with chicken livers or peas.

Mushroom sauce *

Ingredients and quantities for 6 people:

500 g of mushrooms
1 medium onion
2 garlic cloves
1 small bunch of parsley
2 tablespoons olive oil
1 tablespoon lard or fat
2 tablespoons of white wine
salt as needed
pepper as needed

First of all it is important to specify what we mean by mushroom sauce. It is a sauce based on forest mushrooms, typically made with Porcini, but it can also be made with a mixture of Porcini, chanterelle, honey and honey agaric mushrooms, avoiding morel and blackthorn mushrooms only because their taste is very different from the others.

Clean 500 g of mushrooms and dice them finely.

Prepare the base with 1 medium sized onion, 2 chopped garlic cloves, 1 tablespoon of parsley and 1 tablespoon of lard or 2 tablespoons of fat. Brown the vegetables and add the mushrooms on a high flame. Add pepper but not the salt yet, so that the mushrooms don't release water.

When their color starts to change, spray with 2 tablespoons of white wine. As soon as the wine evaporates, add a little water or stock if necessary, in order to avoid that the mushrooms get brown on the outside without being cooked inside.

Then adjust salt and allow to cook on a medium heat until the liquid evaporates. At this point, the greasiest part of the sauce, useful to season the pasta better, will be on the surface.

The mushroom sauce can be used to season *tagliatelle, pappardelle, gramigna, strichetti, garganelli, gnocchi* but not filled pasta. It's perfect with *polenta*.

Peas meat-sauce ✳ ✳

Sauces and seasonings

> **Ingredients and quantities for 6-8 people:**
>
> 250 g onion
> 150 g carrots
> 100 g celery
> 100 g lard
> 500 g beef (shin or neck or brisket)
> 200 g tomato
> 500 g shelled peas
> 1 or 2 glasses of red wine
> salt as needed
> pepper as needed

This meat-sauce is typically prepared at Easter to season *tortelloni* with *ricotta*. Follow the same process as for Bolognese sauce but add peas in the same quantity as meat before adding tomato.

The peas meat-sauce, as well as with *tortelloni*, can be served with any kind of filled pasta.

Peas and ham meat-sauce ✳

> **Ingredients and quantities for 6 people:**
>
> 1 kg peas to be shelled
> 50 g bacon or lard
> 300 g diced cooked ham
> 2 tablespoons of flour
> 1 onion
> 2 garlic cloves
> 2 tablespoons of chopped basil and parsley
> salt as needed
> pepper as needed

Shell the peas: set the shells aside and wash them thoroughly. Prepare a vegetable broth boiling the shells for 30 minutes. Then dispose of the shells and keep the liquid.

Meanwhile, prepare a base for the sauce with 50 g of lard or bacon, 1 onion, 2 garlic cloves and 2 tablespoons of chopped parsley and basil.

Brown and add the peas. Allow to cook for at least 30 minutes. In the meantime, sprinkle with 2 tablespoons of flour, stirring so that it doesn't become

---

The typical product of the Park

Parma ham
The typical and certified Parma ham is produced in the National Park of the river Taro, in the province of Parma.
It is obtained from the legs of pigs, bred for nine months and then butchered, weighing not less than 150 kg. After trimming and salting, the thighs are washed, dried and finally hung and beaten until they achieve their typical round shape. The following stage is the so-called *sugnatura*, in which the whole ham is coated with lard, seasoned with salt and ground pepper.
The ham is not ready for the market, unless it matures for about a year. When cut, it has an even color, between red and pink.
It can be enjoyed fresh with *piadine*, *crescentine* and *tigelle* or it can be used to enrich the filling of fresh egg pasta, such as *tortellini* or modern truffled *tortelloni*.
It's certainly worth remembering its presence in sauces, such as the ham meat sauce, with or without peas.

lumpy. Add salt and pepper. When you have a thick cream, add the diced cooked ham. Add the shells broth until the peas are cooked. Adjust salt and pepper if necessary.

This sauce is very good with *garganelli*, *strichetti* and any kind of simple pasta.

Ham meat-sauce ✳

Ingredients and quantities for 6-8 people:
350 g julienned Parma ham 1 tablespoon of fat butter as needed 200 g tomato purée 1/2 glass of water onion flavor

Prepare the base for the sauce in a pan, rubbing the onion on it. Melt 1 tablespoon of fat, softened with a little butter and add 350 g of Parma ham, finely julienned. Make it warm and then add 200 g of tomato purée with 1/2 glass of water.

Cook for about 10 minutes stirring every now and then and then turn off heat.

The ham sauce is perfect to season *strichetti*, *garganelli* and *straccetti*. It's not very suitable for filled pasta.

Ricotta and spinach sauce ✳

Ingredients and quantities for 6-8 people:
500 g fresh spinach 500 g ricotta 100 g butter 1 glass of fresh whole milk onion flavor salt as needed pepper as needed nutmeg as needed

Clean the spinach, keeping the leaves only, washing them thoroughly many times.

Rub the bottom of the pan with onion and melt 100 g of butter. Add the spinach, still wet after removing them from the water. Adjust salt, pepper and nutmeg.

Allow all the spinach water to evaporate and cook on a medium-low heat, stirring frequently: their size will gradually decrease. Then adjust salt and pepper and check that all the water has evaporated.

Add 500 g of *ricotta*, finely chopped with the mixture until it gets creamy. Add 1 glass of fresh whole milk. The *ricotta* and spinach sauce can be used to season *gnocchi* as well as *ravioli* filled with potatoes or lettuce.

It can be served both with filled and simple pasta, such as *maccheroni*, *sedanini* or *conchiglioni* and *gobetti*. This sauce is not suitable for *tagliatelle* and *pappardelle*.

Giblets meat-sauce ✳ ✳

Ingredients and quantities for 6-8 people:

500 g beef (neck or shin or brisket)
500 g giblets and chicken liver
300 g onion
150 g carrots
100 g celery
100 g lard
1/2 bottle of tomato purée
1 glasses of red wine
salt as needed
pepper as needed

Follow the same process as for Bolognese sauce: in the final stage, before adding tomato, add 500 g of giblets and chicken liver to the 500 g of beef.

It's a richer dish than the traditional Bolognese sauce. This sauce was used to season and fill *lasagne*.

It's perfect on the "white flan" (see recipe on page 60) and very good to season *strichetti*, *garganelli*, *pappardelle*, *strozzapreti* and *gnocchi*.

Sausage meat-sauce *

Ingredients and quantities for 6 people:

350 g sausage
350 g of tomato purée
1 tablespoon of fat or lard
white wine as needed
salt as needed
pepper as needed

Warm 1 tablespoon of fat or lard with 350 g of finely minced sausage. Process it with a tablespoon until it's finely ground. As soon as its color change, add wine, preferably white. Then, add 350 g of tomato purée and boil. Cook for about 1 hour, adding some water every now and then. Before turning off the heat, check if there is a layer of fat on surface, as it can be useful to season the pasta.

The sausage meat-sauce is a very good seasoning for *strichetti*, *garganelli* and *gramigna*.

Gorgonzola cheese sauce *

Ingredients and quantities for 4 people:

70 g sweet gorgonzola cheese
30 g spicy gorgonzola cheese
2 tablespoons of grated parmesan cheese
1 large glass of cream and milk
1 butter knob
salt as needed
pepper as needed

Cook in a bain-marie 70 g of sweet *gorgonzola* cheese and 30 g of spicy *gorgonzola* cheese, 2 tablespoons of grated parmesan cheese, 1 large glass of cream mixed with milk and one knob of butter. Adjust salt and pepper.

Meanwhile cook pasta, drain and mix with the sauce in a bowl: this sauce goes very well with green *gnocchetti* or *conchiglie* or *gobetti*.

Salmon sauce ✻ ✻

Ingredients and quantities for 4 people:

1 dl cream
100 g salmon
30 g parmesan cheese
30 g emmenthal cheese
50 g butter
1 teaspoon of chopped onion
5 tablespoons of white wine
1 tablespoon of cognac
1/2 tablespoon of framboise
salt as needed
pepper as needed

Brown 50 g of butter with the onion very slowly. Spray with 5 tablespoons of white wine and, when it starts boiling, add 1 tablespoon of cognac and 1/2 of framboise, or another raspberry liquor. Blend until creamy and finish with 1 dl of cream and 100 g of diced salmon. Adjust salt and pepper.

When it finishes cooking, add 30 g of parmesan cheese and 30 g of emmenthal cheese and blend thoroughly.

The salmon sauce can be used to season *tagliatelle* and *taglioline*.

Hot sauce for mixed boiled meat ✻

Ingredients and quantities for 6 people:

1 green pepper
1 red pepper
500 g peeled tomatoes
2 garlic cloves
200 g parsley
seed oil as needed
some bread soft part, soaked in vinegar and squeezed
salt as needed
pepper as needed

Chop 2 garlic cloves and 200 g of parsley and brown in the seed oil. Add peppers, a green one and a red one, after chopping them finely. Adjust salt and pepper.

Allow to cook but without browning. Then, add 500 g of peeled tomatoes. Stir and chop the tomatoes and allow to cook for 10-15 minutes more.

Adjust salt and pepper and add the bread, previously soaked in vinegar and squeezed, only at the final cooking minutes. The bread will release the vinegar, helping make a thick cream.

It is important to use only common bread, never bread made with milk or oil.

The hot sauce for mixed boiled meat should be served with all the kinds of meat used for boiling: meat loaf, boiled meat, *cotechino* etc. and can also be served with a grilled T-bone steak or pork chop.

Vegetable sauce ✳

Ingredients and quantities for 6-8 people:

500 g eggplant
500 g zucchini
500 g champignon or field mushrooms
2 garlic cloves
seed or olive oil as needed
fresh marjoram or oregano
salt as needed
pepper as needed

This sauce is prepared with fresh vegetables, preferably with the vegetables in season that can be found from May onwards.

Cut 500 g of champignon or field mushrooms into small pieces. Dice the same amount of eggplants and zucchini (500 g). Prepare a base with oil and brown 2 garlic cloves. Remove the garlic when brown and add vegetable: zucchini, eggplants and mushrooms. Adjust salt and pepper.

Stir continuously until you make a sauce with all the vegetable pieces. At this point, sprinkle thoroughly with chopped fresh marjoram or with oregano. Season the pasta adding some tablespoons of hot water, if necessary.

Complete with a sprinkling of grated parmesan or *pecorino* cheese or salted *ricotta* cheese.

The vegetable sauce can be used to season *strichetti*, *garganelli* as well as *tagliatelle* and *taglioline*.

Clams sauce ✳

Ingredients and quantities for 4 people:

800 g clams
1 tablespoon of chopped onion
1 garlic clove
1 tablespoon of olive oil
white wine as needed
chopped parsley as needed
salt as needed
pepper as needed

Firstly wash 800 g of clams thoroughly. Bang them on a hard surface one by one, with the sharp part downwards. So their shell will open and they can be cleaned in case there is sand in them. This is the only way to avoid spoiling the sauce.

Brown 1 garlic clove in 1 tablespoon of olive oil and then remove it. Stir fry 1 tablespoon of chopped onion, without browning it and add the clams on a low heat. Increase the heat, cover with a lid, and allow to cook. The clams will slowly open. Spray with white wine and sprinkle with chopped fresh parsley. Allow to evaporate.

Let it get cool, remove the shells and then sift the sauce carefully.

Best served with *taglioline*.

Green sauce for mixed boiled meat ✳

Ingredients and quantities for 6-8 people:

1/2 onion
1 garlic clove
200 g parsley
1/2 anchovy in oil
some gherkin in oil
1 boiled potato
1 glass of seed oil
the juice of 1/2 lemon
2 tablespoons vinegar
salt as needed
pepper as needed

Chop 1 garlic clove, 1/2 onion, 200 g of parsley, 1/2 anchovy in oil, some gherkins and stir, adding 1 glass of seed oil little by little. Finally, add 1 boiled potato, to make the sauce thicker. Blend the mix until you get a creamy sauce.

Adjust salt and pepper and finally add the juice of 1/2 lemon and 2 tablespoons of white vinegar.

Serve in cups to use it as a dressing for mixed boiled meat.

Porcini mushrooms sauce ✻

Ingredients and quantities for 6-8 people:

200 g cooked ham
600 g porcini mushrooms
200 g butter
1/2 glass of onion flavored oil
1 garlic clove
1/2 glass of cognac
parsley as needed
1 dash of salt
pepper as needed

Cut 200 g of cooked ham julienne and stir fry with 200 g of butter. Put 1/2 glass of oil of onion (made by soaking 1 tablespoon of chopped onion in 1/2 glass of oil) and 1 garlic clove in a separate pan. Add 1 tablespoon of chopped parsley and stir fry. Add the clean, washed, diced mushrooms and then the julienned ham. Stir and adjust salt. Cook on a high flame until the oil comes back to the surface.

Meanwhile, warm 1/2 glass of cognac in a pan, flame it and pour it immediately in the mushroom pan.

Stir with care and allow to cook for just a few minutes more.

Before seasoning the pasta, add a little warm water to the bowl together with the porcini mushrooms sauce.

This sauce was conceived for seasoning the *paglia and fieno* pasta.

Soups and broth

Soups and broth, too, are among the major dishes of Bolognese cooking.

It is not to be forgotten, by the way, that *tortellini* in broth is one of its traditional classics, a delicate communion of fresh filled pasta and tasty meat stock.

In this section of the book we will make room for some less known recipes very few people have ever heard of.

Stock ✳

Ingredients and quantities for 5 l stock:
800 g beef brisket 2 beef (not veal) knee bones 1 small quarter of a hen (or a Guinea-hen carcass) 1 celery 1 carrot 1 onion salt as needed

When talking about broth, it's important to specify that the ingredients used in making stock for boiled beef – which we will discuss in detail in the chapter about second courses – are essentially different from those required in soup making.

As a matter of fact, soup stock has to enrich the taste of pasta it is served with, and the meat used to cook it is not suitable for a mixed boiled meat dish. Boiled meat liquid (see recipe on page 114) on the other hand, cannot be defined real stock, and is not suitable for soups and broth.

In order to get a good soup stock fill a large pan with cold water, add 800 g of brisket beef, 2 beef knee bones (possibly not veal), a small hen quarter (better if it's a free-range hen!) or a Guinea hen carcass. Add herbs – 1 celery, 1 carrot and 1 onion – season well and simmer over low heat, without skimming fat from surface, for 6 or 7, even 8 hours.

After straining the stock through a sieve, cook pasta in it.

105

Don't forget...

Stock meat
Stock meat can be used for making meatballs, meat and potato stuffing and *ravioli* filling.

Bean soup ✳ ✳

Ingredients and quantities for 6 people:

500 g dried beans
1 onion
4 garlic gloves
1 small bunch of parsley
2 tablespoons of lard (or fat or bacon)
2 large tablespoons of tomato puree (or 1/2 tablespoon of tomato paste)
salt as needed
pepper as needed

Soak beans overnight in plenty of cold water, changing the water several times. The next morning drain and rinse well.

Fill a pan with cold salty water; add 1 onion and the beans. Cook for 1 hour; remove the onion and half beans. Set aside. Puree the remaining beans along with cooking liquid in a vegetable mill. Return to the heat; while bringing to the boil, make a base for the sauce in another saucepan.

Stir in 2 tablespoons of lard (or fat), some chopped parsley leaves and 4 garlic cloves. Cook until brown, not allowing the parsley to overcook. Pour in a ladle of bean stock to stop the cooking process, add 2 large spoonfuls of tomato puree (or 1/2 tablespoon of tomato paste diluted in bean stock).

Dilute with some bean stock if needed, season and cook.

At this stage mix the sauce with the bean stock and cook at low heat for further 40 minutes. After adding the beans formerly set aside, bring slowly to a boil. Plunge the maltagliati in; as soon as they rise to the surface of water turn off and remove from heat. Transfer to a bowl and allow at least 30 minutes standing before serving.

Your bean soup will be excellent even if served lukewarm or cold.

Ciribusla or bean
and polenta soup ✳ ✳

Ingredients and quantities for 6-8 people:

700 g of coarse cornmeal
500 g dry beans
1 onion
4 garlic gloves
1 small bunch of parsley
2 tablespoons of lard (or fat or bacon)
2 large tablespoons of tomato puree (or 1/2 tablespoon
of tomato paste)
salt as needed
pepper as needed

After making a base for the bean soup, add it to the bean stock (as in the previous recipe). Cook for 40 minutes.

In a large pan for 6-8 people (about 6 l capacity) stir 700 g of cornmeal in the stock and cook for further 40 minutes. As soon as cornmeal is ready, turn off heat and plunge in the beans set aside. Pour the bean and *polenta* mixture on a wooden cutting board, then allow cooling for about 10-12 hours. Fit a string under the *polenta* and draw it through to the top, cutting several slices about 2 cm thick. Grill or roast briefly in a frying pan and serve.

Soup in a sack ✳

Ingredients and quantities for 1 person:

for the stock:
1 celery
1 carrot
1 onion
some meaty beef knee or rib bones
salt as needed

for the soup:
30 g flour
1 egg
20 g butter
2 tablespoons of parmesan cheese

1 pinch of salt
nutmeg

for a richer variant:
add 1/2 tablespoon of mortadella

Take 1 celery, 1 carrot, 1 onion and the beef knee or rib bones and make a stock.

Gently stir in 30 g of flour, 1 egg, 20 g of butter and 2 tablespoons of parmesan cheese. Season with a pinch of salt and some grated nutmeg.

Transfer the mixture into a white canvas sack (cotton socks were used once!) tied at one end to a wooden tablespoon put across the edge of the pan. Plunge sack in the pot before turning heat on: make sure it's totally plunged while not touching pan bottom.

Cook for at least 4 hours, remove the sack from pan and transfer the soup into a bowl. Cover it to prevent air from hardening its surface, allow cooling and dice up. Plunge dice into the boiling stock and as soon as they rise to surface, turn off heat. Transfer to a serving bowl.

A tip for a richer variant: add 1/2 tablespoon of *mortadella* to the dough.

Minestrone ✳

Ingredients and quantities for 6 people:

maltagliati (at least 30 g for each person)
1 celery stick
1 carrot
1 onion
1 tablespoon of fat (or olive oil)
1 garlic clove
any vegetables in season (peas, zucchini, potatoes, cabbage, broccoli, spinach, chicory or beetroot)
parsley as needed
basil as needed
salt and pepper as needed

Dice up 1 celery stick, 1 carrot and 1 onion; add 1 garlic clove and stir-fry in 1 tablespoon of fat or vegetable (seed or olive) oil – the latter to be preferred if dish is to be cooked on Christmas' Eve. Make sure herbs do not cook, just lend flavor to the oil or fat.

Fill a pan with cold water, add salt and transfer over heat.

Chop up the vegetables, shell peas and beans, dice up the zucchini and the potatoes, shred cabbage and the broccoli, chop finely spinach, chicory or beetroot along with some parsley and basil leaves.

When water is boiling, plunge in all vegetables and cook for about 1 hour. They are going to be well done by then, but such cooking time is due to get a tastier *minestrone*.

Finally plunge the *maltagliati* (see recipe on page 21) in and as soon as they rise to surface, turn off heat. Allow some standing in a bowl before serving. Your *minestrone* will look and taste differently according to the season.

Tomato soup with straccetti ✳ ✳

Ingredients and quantities for 6 people:
400-450 g straccetti
750 g tomato puree
50 g butter
30-50 parmesan cheese
salt as needed
pepper as needed

Fill a pan with 2.5 l water. Add 750 g of tomato puree and season. When water is boiling, add the garlic and parsley *straccetti* (see recipe on page 81). Serve your tomato soup with 50 g of butter and top generously with parmesan cheese.

Parpadellini with peas * *

Ingredients and quantities for 6 people:

350 g parpadellini
1 kg unshelled peas
1 tablespoon fat or seed oil
1 tablespoon chopped onion
1 garlic clove
2 tablespoons chopped parsley
flour as needed
water as needed
salt as needed
pepper as needed

Lay the dough and cut *parpadellini* into large squares, each side measuring 1.5 cm. Make sure your pastry is thinner than that for *tortelloni* (see recipe on page 27).

Shell peas; set pods aside and cook them in water for about 1/2 hour to get a light vegetable stock.

In another frying-pan, make a base for the sauce with 1 tablespoon of fat (use seed or olive oil if dish is to be served on Christmas' Eve), 1 tablespoon of chopped onion and 1 garlic clove or shallot.

When ready, add peas and sprinkle with flour. Stir quickly to avoid lumping and when flour has browned add the pod stock. Allow cooking for at least 40 minutes (cooking time depending on pea size). Taste before seasoning and adding 350 g of *parpadellini*.

Turn off heat as soon as *parpadellini* rise to surface, sprinkle with 2 tablespoons of fresh chopped parsley and mix well while the latter gets cooked through soup warmth.

Parpadellini and pea soup is also excellent served warm and will perfectly suit a buffet dinner.

Don't forget...

Run out of onion and garlic?
Whenever a recipe includes onion and garlic among its ingredients, these can be replaced with shallot if necessary; this rule can be applied always.

Passatelli *

Ingredients and quantities for 6 people:

100 g flour
300 g fine breadcrumbs
300 g parmesan cheese
7 eggs
1,8 l of stock
salt and nutmeg as needed

Don't forget...

Bread for passatelli
When making *passatelli*, it's better to crumble common or Tuscany bread. Avoid olive oil or milk bread, as they will cause *passatelli* to melt into hot stock while cooking.

Mix 300 g of finely crumbled bread, 300 g of parmesan cheese, 7 eggs and season with salt and nutmeg. Make a well with 100 g of flour and mix ingredients by hand until they bind together.

You shouldn't handle dough too long; try to knead it at least half an hour before cooking in order to allow ingredients to combine well.

Then use a *schiacciapassatelli* (or a more common potato masher!), to make the *passatelli*: place the potato mixture in the masher and gently squeeze it over the pan, so as to drop the *passatelli* straight into boiling stock.

Remove from heat as soon as they rise to surface, and serve.

Tortellini in stock * * *

Ingredients for 6-8 people:

for the dough:
4 eggs
400 g of flour

for the filling:
100 g of mortadella
100 g of pork loin
100 g of Parma ham
100 g of grated parmesan cheese
1 egg
1 knob of butter
1 pinch of salt
1,8 l of stock
wine as needed
nutmeg as needed

For the *tortellini* filling, follow the traditional recipe (page 89) to get a smooth mixture with medium consistency and moisture.

Knead 4 eggs and 400 g of flour as suggested in the traditional pastry recipe (see recipe on page 13): the pastry for your tortellini should be as thin as a veil. After wrapping the filling and shaping your *tortellini*, plunge them into boiling stock. Remove from heat as soon as they rise to surface.

Allow standing before serving.

Imperial soup *

Ingredients and quantities for 6 people:

60 g butter
4 eggs
50 g semolina flour
60 g parmesan cheese
salt as needed
salt and nutmeg as needed

Whip 4 eggs and a pinch of salt until getting a delicate foam. Once it's firm and soft, add 50 g of semolina flour and 60 g of grated parmesan cheese. Season with salt and nutmeg and mix ingredients until they bind well.

Pour 60 g of melted butter into a wide shallow tin, add mixture and bake at 180° for 10-15 minutes. Allow cooling; cut into strips about 1 cm wide, then dice strips up.

Cook in hot boiling stock, and when dice rise to surface your Imperial soup is ready.

Meat-based second courses

Notwithstanding a common opinion which sees Bolognese cooking as the exclusive kingdom of superb first courses, its tradition provides a whole range of tasty second courses usually based on pork, beef, veal, chicken, turkey, lamb and rabbit meat.

Among these, the most renowned ones feature meats boiled with vegetables, roasted in various fashion or formed into meatballs, as well as bread crumb dredged cutlets, stews and stuffed zucchini.

Roast pork ✳ ✳

Ingredients and quantities for 4 people:

1 kg capocollo (prime cuts of pork meat) or shoulder or boneless meat
fat as needed
garlic as needed
rosemary as needed
white whine as needed
salt and pepper as needed

Roast pork is to be cooked in the oven. You will get the best results using either *capocollo* or the shoulder, but it's very important to tie pork meat well with a string, adding salt, pepper, garlic and rosemary into the net. Stir-fry in a non-sticking pan previously coated with fat; when meat gets golden brown sprinkle with white whine and transfer to a roasting tin. Pour enough wine and stock to half-cover meat. Turn it every now and then in order to cook each side, cover with a tin foil and roast in the oven at 180° for 1 hour.

Allow cooling, remove string and slice. Reheat with sauce and serve.

The typical product of the Park

The dark pork race from Romagna
This is a local pork race, which is disappearing unfortunately. Its main weakness are two.
This kind of pork grows slowlier than the marketed *large white* race. Moreover, its meats is very fat, which does not meet with the contemporary market requirements that prefer "lean" pork meat".
For these reasons, the dark pork race has been almost forgotten to make space for the development of industrial pork breeding. This kind of tender meat, like the local bovine race, is very suitable for the Bolognese cooking recipes, which require this tasty ingredient, such as the famous *tortellini* filling, ribs, stewed or roast pork and many delicious cold meats and sausages.

Roast veal ✳ ✳

Ingredients and quantities for 4 people:

1 kg veal belly or brisket
1 carrot
1 celery
1 onion
garlic as needed
rosemary as needed
fat as needed
white whine as needed
salt as needed
pepper as needed

Choose some good veal belly or brisket. Rub it with salt and pepper, add garlic and rosemary. Pan roast it carefully on each side, then sprinkle generously with white wine; add 1 carrot, 1 celery and 1 onion and place in the oven. Cover with wine and stock.

Allow cooking for about 1 hour, allow cooling and slice. When your guests are having starters, reheat along with sauce for about 30 minutes and then serve.

Mixed boiled meats ✳ ✳

Ingredients and quantities for 10-12 people:

1.2 kg beef meat (even low quality will do)
1 kg various meats (veal or beef tongue, veal or pig trotters, veal head, breasts and tail)
1 cotechino or 1 zampone
1 chicken (weighing about 1 kg)
1 carrot
1 onion
1 celery
salt as needed

The first rule to succeed in cooking this dish is choosing the right meats: some beef (even low quality meat will do), a veal or beef tongue, veal or pig trotters, the chicken, a veal head, some *cotechino* or *zampone*, and even breasts (commonly known as *latte*, "milk") and a tail.

Boil each type of meat on its own, along with some celery, carrot, onion and a pinch of salt (tail and tongue only may be cooked together). Plunge the meats in hot boiling water, not in cold water as in soup stock (see recipe on page 105). The main difference between boiled meats and meat stock cooking processes, in fact, is that in the former meat is plunged into hot boiling water which immediately closes its pores, thus saving its taste; in the latter, instead the cold water allows meat to lend its flavor to the stock.

Each kind of meat will require boiling for at least 3 or 4 hours, with just chicken being ready in about 2 hours.

Zampone is to be cooked in a dedicated saucepan, the *zamponiera*, and has to be previously soaked in water overnight due to its thick skin. It requires about 4 hour cooking.

Cotechino can be cooked in a common saucepan, but do not forget to insert toothpicks to prevent it from touching the pan bottom and tearing its delicate membrane. Add 1 bay leaf at will. Allow boiling for about 1 and 1/2 hour.

Your mixed boiled meat dish must be prepared several hours before serving. Allow cooling, then slice and reheat each meat in its own stock.

Serve along with stock and sauces (for suitable sauces see recipe on pages 101 and 103).

Don't forget...

The main rule for any cook is to taste their dishes before serving. So the cook can still adjust salt and pepper if necessary before the guests try it.

Milk pork chops ✳

Ingredients and quantities for 6 people:

6 chops (no tenderloin)
1 tablespoon flour
1 tablespoon of fat
2 tablespoons stock
milk as needed
salt as needed
pepper as needed

Season 6 pork chops on both sides with salt and pepper.

Preheat a deep non-sticking frying pan and melt 1 tablespoon of fat; when this gets to its smoking point add the chops. As soon as they're browning on both sides, add milk until covering chops and cook at medium heat until milk gets absorbed. Chops must be placed all around pan bottom and completely soaked in milk. When this finally curdles, remove chops from pan and transfer to a serving dish.

Place pan back over heat, add 2 tablespoons of stock and 1 tablespoon of flour. Cook until the mixture thickens and pour it over chops before serving.

Fried lamb ribs ✳

From a hearty tradition

Easter day was usually spent at home with one's closest relatives, grandparents and uncles. A typical Easter menu would feature ricotta cheese *tortelloni* with peas, along with a stock soup (usually *tortellini* in stock). The most common second course would be lamb ribs, dredged in bread crumbs and then fried, and veal in a tuna sauce. Easter dinner would usually culminate in a *pinza* or a *ciambella pasquale* (one of the several fashion this typical ring-shaped cake is made in Bologna).

Ingredients and quantities for 4-5 people:

20 lamb ribs (4 ribs per person)
1 tablespoon grated parmesan cheese
2 tablespoons of fresh liquid cream
4 eggs
flour as needed
bread crumbs as needed
salt as needed
pepper as needed
nutmeg as needed

Lay ribs on a tray, seasoning both sides with salt and pepper. Set aside.

Mix 4 eggs, 1 tablespoon of parmesan cheese, 2 tablespoons of fresh liquid cream, salt, pepper and nutmeg. Dredge each rib first in the flour, then in the egg mixture, and finally coat with bread crumbs.

Make sure rib bones stay clean, in order to use them to handle ribs; alternatively, wrap them with tin foil.

Bolognese cutlets ✳ ✳

Ingredients and quantities for 6 people:

3 eggs
1 tablespoon of grated parmesan cheese
80 g slivered parmesan cheese
1 tablespoon of fresh liquid cream
600 g pork (pork loin)
200 g Parma ham
1/2 cup meat stock
some drops of liquid cream for the icing
bread crumbs as needed
fat as needed
salt as needed
pepper as needed
nutmeg as needed

in addition:
white truffle

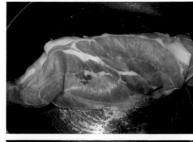

Mix 3 eggs with 1 tablespoon of parmesan cheese, salt, pepper, nutmeg and 1 tablespoon of fresh cream. Set aside.

Cut the pork loin into slices about 1/2 cm thick. Dredge slices in flour, then in the egg mixture, and finally in bread crumbs. Fry in fat; when golden transfer each cutlet to another non-sticking frying pan, without drying it in roll paper.

Lay 1-2 slices of Parma ham and some slivered parmesan cheese on each cutlet, pouring a drop of liquid cream over the parmesan to soften it.

Pour 2 tablespoons of meat stock, close but not on top of cutlet. Cover with lid and turn heat off. Garnish with a sprinkle of white truffle.

Though apparently easy to make, Bolognese cutlets require plenty of ingredients and a careful preparation.

Mortadella cutlets *

Ingredients and quantities for 1 person:

1 thick mortadella slice
1/2 egg per person
milk as needed
bread crumbs as needed
salt as needed
pepper as needed

Cut the *mortadella* into a 1 cm thick slice, trimming it into a square or a triangle; alternatively, you may leave its oval shape and cut it into smaller portions at time of serving. Soak in milk, covered, for 15-20 minutes. Set aside.

Mix eggs, salt and pepper (less ingredients than in the Bolognese cutlet are required due to the strong flavor of the *mortadella*).

Dredge the *mortadella* in bread crumbs, then in the eggs and once more in the bread crumbs.

In order to get a good coating, allow cutlets to stand in bread crumbs for about 5-10 minutes, turning them once. This is essential in order to prevent fat from spoiling the flavor of the *mortadella* during the frying process.

Meat pie ✳

Ingredients and quantities for 6-8 people:

for the pastry:
500 g flour
1 egg
100 g fat
10 g salt
water as needed

for the filling:
500 g meat
100 g mortadella
100 g parmesan cheese (at will)
2 eggs
500 g boiled potatoes
vegetables (spinach, asparagus, potatoes)
salt and pepper as needed
nutmeg as needed

Mix 500 g of flour, 100 g of fat and a pinch of salt. Make a well with the mixture and add 1 egg in the centre. Knead well until ingredients combine.

Divide the pastry in two parts, one twice as big as the other: use the bigger part as pie base, placing it on the bottom of a 30 cm wide flan tin; use the remaining part as pie lid after laying the filling.

It's now time to prepare the vegetables and meat you need for the filling; this usually made with boiled and roast meat, as well as stew leftovers, spinach, asparagus and other vegetables. Add boiled potatoes to the meat and *mortadella*. Mince and season with salt, pepper, nutmeg and 2 eggs. At will, add 100 g of parmesan cheese to enrich the mixture.

After laying the filling in a flan tin, cover it with the round-shaped pastry lid; seal pie edges by pressing gently but firmly with a fork or fingers. Make several cuts on the pastry with a sharp knife, brush with milk or water and bake at 160° for 40 minutes.

Usually served hot, your meat pie will taste as good presented lukewarm.

Potato pie ✳

Ingredients and quantities for 6-8 people:

1 kg boiled potatoes
200 g parmesan cheese
2 eggs
100 g butter
150 g finely sliced salami or pork sausage
50 g parmesan cheese
butter flakes
salt as needed
nutmeg as needed
breadcrumbs as needed

Plunge potatoes into salted boiling water without overcooking them. Peel, mash and reheat.

Stir in 200 g of parmesan cheese, 2 eggs and 100 g of butter; combine well and adjust salt and nutmeg. Butter a tin flan, sprinkling generously with crumbled breads; then use a spatula or simply your hands to spread a 1 cm thick layer of the potato mixture.

Now spread a layer of finely sliced salami, thoroughly covering previous layer. Stop when you'll have 3 potato and 2 salami layers; finally sprinkle an abundance of butter flakes and parmesan cheese.

Roast in the oven at 160°-180° for about 30-40 minutes and serve lukewarm.

Pan roast chicken, guinea-fowl or rabbit ✳

Ingredients and quantities for 4 people:

1,2-1,5 kg chicken or rabbit or guinea-fowl
garlic as needed
rosemary as needed
fat as needed
white whine as needed
salt as needed
pepper as needed

Singe and divide the chicken or the guinea-fowl in parts – wings, breast, thighs, breast and back – following their joints. Chop the rabbit in 8 parts.

Wash the chicken, guinea-fowl or rabbit under cold water; then season with a pinch of salt and pepper, garlic and rosemary.

Brown gently the meat in an iron roasting pan over medium-low heat, add 1 tablespoon of fat and cover with lid. When it gets well browned, add some white whine, turning heat off as soon as this evaporates.

Chicken and guinea-fowl will take 30-40 minutes to cook, while rabbit at least 45-50. When the meat browns, spray with white wine, allow to evaporate and turn off heat. Present on a serving dish.

Chicken cacciatore ✳

Ingredients and quantities for 6-8 people:

1 chicken weighing about 1.5 kg
1 kg sauce tomatoes
1 tablespoon of lard or fat
3 onions
2 or 3 garlic cloves
some rosemary leaves

> salt as needed
> pepper as needed
> 1 glass of white wine

Singe and chop chicken, leaving thighs and wings whole. Lay it in a bowl, adding 2 or 3 garlic cloves and some rosemary leaves. Season with salt and pepper.

In a casserole melt 1 tablespoon of lard or fat and add chopped meat without the herbs.

Cook at medium-high heat, stirring frequently and adding a full glass of white whine.

In the meantime, finely slice 1 kg of sauce tomatoes and 3 onions; lay them on chopped meat, cover and cook at medium-low heat, so as to have vegetables lending flavor to the chicken.

After 15-20 minutes remove lid and mix carefully.

Allow sauce to dry up just slightly, as it will get thicker even when heat is turned off.

Grandma Carla's meatballs *

> **Ingredients and quantities for 6-8 people:**
>
> 1 kg pork meat (not loin)
> 100 g mortadella
> 150 g grated parmesan cheese
> 2 tablespoons bread crumbs soaked in milk
> 3 eggs
> bread crumbs as needed
> fat or seed oil
> salt as needed
> pepper as needed
> nutmeg as needed

Mince 1 kg of pork meat and 100 g of *mortadella* at least twice. Add 150 g of grated parmesan cheese, 3 eggs, 2 tablespoons of bread crumbs soaked in milk and season with salt, pepper and nutmeg.

Form meatballs and dredge them gently, one by one, into bread crumbs: be careful not to squash them, then lay into a preheated pan with seed oil (or even better, in fat) to brown.

They are ready when they don't release blood anymore and, at the same time, are still soft.

Peas and meatballs ✳

Ingredients and quantities for 6-8 people:

1 kg minced pork meat (breast, not loin)
150 g mortadella
100 g finely minced Parma ham
300 g parmesan cheese
2 tablespoons bread crumbs soaked in milk
3 eggs
1 tomato sauce
1 tablespoon chopped onion
white whine as needed
1 kg of unshelled peas
salt as needed
pepper as needed
nutmeg as needed
fat as needed

To make meatballs, mince at least twice meat pork and *mortadella*; add grated parmesan cheese, eggs, bread crumbs soaked in milk and season with salt, pepper and nutmeg. Form meatballs and dredge them one by one into flour, being careful not to smash them.

Brown 1 tablespoon of minced onion in a preheated pan with fat; add the meatballs, turning them once or covering with lid. Sprinkle generously with white whine, which combined with meatballs flour will make a tasty sauce. Before this evaporates completely, add a bottle of tomato sauce. As soon as mixture starts boiling again, stir in the shelled peas and cook for about 45 minutes. Season with salt and pepper before serving.

If needed, add some stock or milk to prevent your meatballs from getting too dry.

Meat loaf ✽

Ingredients and quantities for 6-8 people:

1 kg minced pork meat (not loin)
150 g mortadella
100 g Parma ham
300 g parmesan cheese
3 eggs
1 boiled egg
2 boiled carrots
salt as needed
pepper as needed
nutmeg as needed

Don't forget...

Never use tin foil for your meatloaf...!
Always use a tea cloth, not a tin foil, to get a successful meatloaf: this won't allow stock to filter, and the meat will not cook properly.

Mix together 1 kg of minced pork, 150 g of *mortadella*, 300 g of grated parmesan cheese, 3 eggs, salt, pepper and nutmeg. Set aside.

Boil the carrots and dice the Parma ham. Before laying the mixture on a white tea cloth, add the diced Parma ham and mix well. Roll the dough; top with the previously chopped boiled carrots and eggs. Wrap in a tea cloth, sealing carefully. Since there are so many finely chopped ingredients, you should try it to form a meat loaf at least 15 cm wide.

Meat loaf has to be cooked in stock: not necessarily meat stock, but also a simple vegetable one (known as *brodo matto* in some parts of Italy), made with carrots, celery, onion and 1 pinch of salt. Boil for 1 hour and a half, remove from heat and allow cooling or, better, refrigerating overnight. It tastes even better if prepared the day before.

Serve meatloaf after reheating in its stock; serve sliced and hot, sided by sauces for mixed boiled meat (see recipe on pages 101 and 103).

The typical product of the Park

The race from Romagna)

It has very ancient and geographically far origins: the story goes about this bovine race that originally was in China, then in Mongolia, East Europe and finally arrived to *Romagna* in the 4th century A.D., by means of the Lombard army. Most of the animals of this race are still grown in pastures. They are butchered between 11 and 18 moths of age, as soon as the animals weigh around 600-700 kg.

The *romagnola* race has been awarded the IGP (Protected geographic recommendation) with the following name: "White veal of the Central Apennine IGP". Its top quality meat can be used in many ways. Perfect for stock, stewed beef and Bolognese sauce.

Stew ✽

Ingredients and quantities for 6 people:

1 kg pork meat (not loin) or beef or veal (chuck or shoulder)

---

150 g bacon or minced fat
2 onions
1 glass of red wine
750 g tomato sauce
1 kg potatoes
flour as needed
some rosemary leaves
2 garlic cloves
salt as needed
pepper as needed

Stew can be cooked both with pork or beef: you do not have to necessarily use prime cuts, even chuck or shoulder will do. Some people would use veal, even if its not very tasty.

Chop 1 kg of meat into small, even pieces. Transfer to a bowl, season with salt, pepper, 2 garlic cloves and some rosemary leaves. Set aside.

On a preheated pan lay 150 g of minced bacon or fat and 2 onions; sprinkle meat with flour, add to pan and brown.

Sprinkle with red wine and let evaporate; add 750 g of tomato sauce, then, after about 1/2 hour, 1 kg of chopped potatoes. Add stock in ladles while cooking for 30-40 minutes more.

Don't forget...

Roasting pan
A well equipped kitchen can never miss an iron pan used exclusively to roast meat.
Never wash it with soap: rub gently with roll paper and a pinch of salt.
This way it will retain the smell of roasted meat and a veil of cooked fat which will render it naturally a non-sticking pan.

Spareribs ✳

Ingredients and quantities for 4 people:

1 kg pork spareribs
1 tablespoon of fat
3-4 garlic cloves
rosemary
white whine as needed
salt as needed
pepper as needed

After seasoning spareribs generously with salt and pepper, transfer them to a preheated iron pan with a veil of fat or lard. Cover and brown over medium-high heat.

Add 3 or 4 garlic cloves along with some rosemary leaves. Sprinkle with white wine: when sauce thickens your spareribs are done.

Veal with tuna sauce ✳ ✳

Ingredients for 6-8 people:

700 g of veal silverside or breast

for the stock:
1 celery
1 carrot
1 onion
1 glass of white whine

for the tuna sauce:
500 g tuna
2 anchovy fillets in olive oil
1 tablespoon of capers
3 eggs
1 glass of seed oil
1 tablespoon of vinegar
juice of 1/2 lemon
salt as needed
pepper as needed

In a big stock pan, put water, 1 glass of white whine, 1 celery, 1 carrot and 1 onion.

Tie carefully 700 g of silverside (or veal breast) and plunge it into boiling water. Cook for about 2 hours, but don't let meat lose its tenderness.

In the meantime, make the tuna sauce mixing 500 g of tuna with 2 anchovy fillets in olive oil, 1 tablespoon of capers, 3 eggs, 1 glass of seed oil, juice of 1/2 lemon and 1 tablespoon of vinegar. Adjust salt and pepper.

Cut the veal in thin slices; layer them on a tray, spreading generously the tuna sauce over each layer (don't make more than three, though).

Refrigerate for several hours to serve cold.

Stuffed zucchini *

Ingredients and quantities for 6 people:

1 kg zucchini
1 level tablespoon of fat
1 bottle tomato sauce
7 dl milk
butter flakes

for the stuffing:
300 g pork (not loin)
30 g mortadella
40 g grated parmesan cheese
1 tablespoon of bread crumbs soaked in milk
1 egg
salt as needed
pepper as needed
nutmeg as needed

Don't forget...

Zucchini filling
If after stuffing zucchini you still have some left-over filling, use it to make some meatballs to cook along.
Use the remaining pulp to prepare a tasty omelet.

The filling used in this recipe is the same mixture used to make meatballs: 300 g of pork, 30 g of *mortadella*, 40 g of grated parmesan, 1 egg, 1 tablespoon of bread crumbs soaked in milk, salt, pepper and nutmeg.

Scoop out the zucchini pulp and fill in the stuffing. Put 1 level tablespoon of fat in a casserole; lay the zucchini, and allow them to brown on every side. Add a bottle of tomato sauce and 7 dl of milk. Adjust salt and pepper and garnish with cold butter flakes. Cover and cook over medium heat. When the mixture starts boiling, lower the heat and cook for further 30 minutes, occasionally turning the zucchini.

Side dishes and more

Traditionally, there are dishes that cannot be listed in the typical main and second courses. This chapter illustrates those delicacies that can become real main courses in certain occasions, as well as the classical vegetable side dishes. You will learn about the *friggione*, enriched with sausage bits, the potato roll with *radicchio*, porcini mushrooms or spinach, the stewed eggs with spinach, the eggplants *Parmigiana*, the vegetable fritters and the filled peppers. These are more than just side dishes.

As a complement to the previous chapter we will also suggest the right matching with fresh season vegetables, gratin, fried and stewed, baked or cooked in a pan.

Artichokes casserole ✳

Ingredients and quantities for 6 people:

6 artichokes
butter flakes
1 tablespoon of olive oil
salt as needed
pepper as needed

Clean the artichokes, cut them into segments and keep the stalks. Lay them on a baking pan after pouring a lot of cold water. Season with salt and pepper and add 1 tablespoon of olive oil. Sprinkle with butter flakes.

Cook on heat, covering with greaseproof paper or with a lid. Uncover after 20 minutes and turn the artichokes upside down. Allow to dry until they brown.

Fried cardoons ✳

Ingredients and quantities for 6 people:

semolina as needed
1 kg cardoons

fat (or seed oil) as needed
salt as needed

Buy straight, white cardoons. Clean them, cutting off the ends and peeling both sides of the stalks. Chop into 5-7 cm long sticks and soak in cold water.

Cook in salted boiling water for about 10-15 minutes. Strain and dry carefully with a towel or with roll paper.

Meanwhile, prepare a frying pan and melt 1 tablespoon of fat (or seed oil). Coat the cardoon sticks, one by one, with semolina, shake them and then plunge them in hot fat. Fry them, turning them on one side and the other. Remove when crispy and lay on a serving dish, sprinkling with 1 dash of salt.

Gratin of cardoons ✳

Ingredients and quantities for 6 people:

1.2 kg cardoons
butter as needed
grated parmesan cheese as needed
nutmeg as needed

for the béchamel sauce:
3 l milk
25 g butter
15 g flour
salt as needed
nutmeg as needed

Prepare the béchamel sauce (see recipe on p. 90).

Clean the cardoons thoroughly and cut them into 5-7 cm long sticks: while the previous recipe requires straight cardoons, it is advisable to use the bended ones for this recipe, as they are more fleshy. Wash them in cold water. Cook in salted boiling water and put in a baking pan, previously greased with butter and with a thin layer of béchamel sauce. Sprinkle with grated parmesan cheese and nutmeg. Bake gratin for about half an hour.

Stewed cardoons ✳

Ingredients and quantities for 6 people:

1 kg cardoons
2 tablespoons of olive oil
2 garlic cloves
1 small bunch of parsley
300 g of tomato purée
salt as needed
pepper as needed

Choose curved cardoons, clean them and soak in cold water until they get darker. Prepare a base with 2 tablespoons of olive oil, 2 garlic cloves, a small bunch of parsley and allow to brown.

Then, add 300 g of tomato purée, the cardoons and as much water as needed to cover everything. Cook for about half an hour on a medium-low heat and adjust salt and pepper before serving.

Baked onions ✳

Ingredients and quantities for 6 people:

6 white onions
fat as needed
some rosemary leaves
olive oil
1/2 glass of white wine
salt as needed
pepper as needed

Choose 6 big white onions. Cut them in two halves horizontally and lay them on a baking dish previously greased with fat or olive oil. Season with salt and pepper and sprinkle with some rosemary leaves. Pour a little olive oil on the onions, add a little water and white wine, without covering completely.

Bake at 180° for 20-30 minutes.

The onions are ready when the middle part rises. Serve with their own sauce.

Bitter-sweet baby onions *

Ingredients and quantities for 4 people:
500 g baby onions 1 tablespoon of seed oil 1 teaspoon of sugar white or red wine as needed salt as needed pepper as needed

Peel 500 g of baby onions, removing the thin outer peel and the roots with a knife.

Then blanch for 3-5 minutes while preparing a frying pan with 1 tablespoon of seed oil and 1 tablespoon of sugar, which need to caramelize on the heat.

As soon as the caramel is ready, add the baby onions with a little amount of their own water. Adjust salt and pepper. Stir with care and add a little more water if necessary. Cover with a lid and allow to cook for 10 minutes. Before they are ready, remove the lid and allow the liquid to evaporate. Spray with white or red wine and turn off the heat.

Allow to rest a few minutes before serving.

Gratin of fennels *

Ingredients and quantities for 6 people:
1 kg fennels 0.5 l béchamel sauce 50 g parmesan cheese
summer version: 100 g butter 50 g of parmesan cheese a sprinkling of nutmeg

Clean and wash the fennels. Cut them into segments and soak in a pan with salted cold water. Put the pan on the heat and bring to boil. Remove from the heat when they are cooked, that is when the border is transparent and the inside is white, and allow to cool.

To make the classic version of this dish, grease a baking dish with butter and put the fennels on it, covering them with 0.5 l of béchamel sauce (see recipe on page 90) and 50 g of parmesan cheese.

To make the summer version, use 100 g of melted butter instead of the béchamel sauce, with 50 g of parmesan cheese and a sprinkling of nutmeg.

Bake gratin for 15 minutes and serve.

Friggione ✳

> **Ingredients and quantities for 6-8 people:**
>
> 1 kg onion
> 1 kg ripe tomatoes
> 1 tablespoon seed oil
> salt as needed
>
> **in addition:**
> peppers
> sausage

Slice 1 kg of onions and 1 kg of ripe tomatoes. Pour 1 tablespoon of seed oil in a deep pan and add onion and tomato without heating, seasoning with 1 dash of salt. Allow to cook on a medium-low heat, covering with a lid, for 30 minutes.

The *friggione* is ready when the vegetables are cooked and, if still watery, allow to dry letting it rest without heating.

You can also add peppers, but only if they are in season and in the same quantity as onion or tomato. It is also possible to enrich this dish with small sausage cubes, added to the rest of the ingredients at the beginning of the cooking process.

It is advisable to cook *friggione* a few hours before serving, thus allowing time to get thicker and tastier. This dish, with the additional sausage, can be served as a second course.

The typical product of the Park

The salsiccia matta (mad sausage) or *ciavar* and the sambudello romagnolo
Nothing in the pork goes wasted. Thus, both the *salsiccia matta*, or *ciavar*, and the *sambudello romagnolo* are the result of the processing of less fine pork meat cuts: tongue, heart, cheeks and offals, set aside after boning the head.
In the case of *sambudello romagnolo,* these parts are previously minced and then mixed with salt, pepper and abundant garlic. In the case of *ciavar*, on the other hand, the mixture is enriched with *sangiovese* (red) wine, which enhances its taste. Both can be grilled or matured and stored in oil.
They are delicious if served with small bits of fried *polenta*.
The *ciavar* is perfect for enriching the tasty *friggione*.

Vegetable fritters ✷ ✷

Ingredients and quantities for 6 people:

90 g flour
500 g chicory and beet
90 g grated parmesan cheese
3 eggs
1/2 glass of milk
frying fat
salt as needed
pepper as needed
nutmeg as needed

Prepare 500 g of chicory and beet. Clean the vegetables and dice them into 2-3 cm pieces. Cook in salted boiling water. After straining with care, put in a bowl wit salt, pepper, nutmeg and 90 g of grated parmesan cheese.

Prepare the batter separately, mixing 90 g of flour, 3 eggs and 1/2 glass of milk. Blend with the vegetables and make a single mix.

Then put a layer of fat in a frying pan and fry the fritters on both sides.

Dry on roll paper and sprinkle with salt. They can be served both hot and cold. For this reason, they are perfect for buffets, picnics and country parties.

Eggplants Parmigiana ✷ ✷

Ingredients and quantities for 6 people:

150 g grated parmesan cheese
100 g full-cream mozzarella

for fried eggplants:
flour as needed
1 kg eggplants
frying seed oil and salt as needed
salt as needed

for the tomato sauce:
1 tablespoon of seed oil
2 garlic cloves
1 bottle of tomato purée

> 1 small bunch of chopped basil
> salt as needed
> pepper as needed
>
> **in addition:** cooked ham

Slice 1 kg of eggplants, approximately 3 or 4 big ones. Cut them into 1 cm thick slices. Soak in salted cold water for at least half an hour.

Remove from the water and dry with care; coat with flour and then fry them in a non-sticking pan with 1 tablespoon of seed oil. Lay on a roll paper sheet to dry.

Meanwhile, prepare the tomato sauce. Make a base with 2 garlic cloves and 1 tablespoon of seed oil. Allow to brown and then remove the garlic. At this point, add a bottle of tomato purée and a small bunch of chopped basil. Adjust salt and pepper and allow to cook, adding some water if too thick.

Put a layer of eggplants in a baking dish and top with the tomato sauce, a sprinkling of grated parmesan cheese and the full-cream mozzarella (diced or grated), then some more tomato sauce, another layer of eggplants and so on, making at least three layers of eggplants.

Finish with abundant parmesan cheese and mozzarella. Bake for about 20 minutes.

Another version of this dish includes a layer of cooked ham before adding parmesan cheese and mozzarella.

Stringy potatoes ✳

> **Ingredients and quantities for 6-8 people:**
>
> 1 kg potatoes
> 1 l milk
> grated parmesan cheese as needed
> salt as needed
> nutmeg as needed

Wash and peel potatoes. Slice them finely and put on a baking dish until you cover the whole surface.

Cover with cold milk and season with salt and

nutmeg. Bake for 40-45 minutes, after covering the baking dish with a lid or with tin foil.

Halfway through cooking time, when potatoes get softer, uncover and add grated parmesan cheese. Turn off when they are well baked and the parmesan cheese becomes stringy.

Stringy potatoes are served with their own cooking milk sauce.

Filled peppers ✻

Ingredients and quantities for 6 people:

6 medium-sized peppers
50 g butter
salt as needed

for the filling:
600 g ground pork (not loin)
80 g mortadella
60 g ground Parma ham
140 g parmesan cheese
2 eggs
salt as needed
pepper as needed
nutmeg as needed

Wash 6 medium-sized peppers thoroughly, better if yellow and red and remove the footstalk, the heart and the seeds. Mince 600 g of pork, 80 g of *mortadella*, 60 g of Parma ham, 140 g of parmesan cheese, 2 eggs, salt, pepper and nutmeg and blend. This filling can be used to fill peppers.

Then put the filled peppers on a deep pan, with a base of melted butter and some butter flakes on top. Cover the pan with tin foil and allow to cook on a low heat for 40-45 minutes. Adjust taste with a few grains of coarse salt.

Turn the filled peppers on all sides and add a little water if necessary. Actually, this could be a proper second course: tasty, creative and nourishing.

Peas with ham ✳

Ingredients and quantities for 6 people:

1 tablespoon of flour
1 kg of unshelled peas
2 garlic cloves
1 medium-sized onion
100 g of cooked ham
vegetable stock or water
seed oil as needed
salt as needed
pepper as needed

Don't forget...

How to use the discarded parts of peas
After boiling the shelled peas, keep the water and plunge the shells into it. Let them cook and overcook: then remove them and keep the liquid.
Make it thicker with a little butter and flour, mixing the ingredients with care, you will get a peas cream to be served with croutons: a delicious solution to save the nutritious properties of pea-shells!

Shell 1 kg of peas and cook in boiling water, slightly salted, for about 20 minutes. Meanwhile, use a deep pan to prepare a base with seed oil, 2 garlic cloves, 1 medium-sized onion and brown these vegetables. Spray with some white wine if necessary.

Then, add the peas and allow to season. Sprinkle with a little flour and allow to cook. Stir and cover with vegetable stock or water (best with the peas cooking water). Cook on a medium-low heat until the peas are completely cooked. Let the sauce get thicker.

Finally, add 100 g of diced cooked ham and adjust salt and pepper.

Gratin of tomatoes ✳

Ingredients and quantities for 6 people:

6 red round tomatoes
2 tablespoons of breadcrumbs
3-4 tablespoons of parmesan cheese
2 chopped garlic cloves
1 small bunch of chopped parsley
olive oil as needed
salt as needed
pepper as needed

Wash 6 red, round tomatoes; cut them into two halves and remove the seeds and the saucy flesh to be set aside. Season each half with a dash of salt and lay them on a baking dish, previously greased with oil.

Meanwhile, mix the saucy flesh and the seeds with 2 tablespoons of breadcrumbs, 4-5 tablespoons of parmesan cheese, salt and pepper and 2 chopped garlic cloves and a small bunch of parsley. Blend the mixture until creamy; fill the tomatoes and top with a little olive oil.

Add 2 tablespoons of water and cover the baking dish. Bake at 180° for 15 minutes. Uncover and allow to brown a little more, sprinkling with parmesan cheese or breadcrumbs.

Mash potatoes *

Ingredients and quantities for 6 people:

1 kg potatoes
2 glasses of milk
100 g butter
salt as needed
nutmeg as needed

in addition:
1 yolk
grated parmesan cheese

Cook 1 kg of washed potatoes in salted boiling water without peeling them. When they are ready, peel them and mash them with a potato-masher at least two times.

In the meantime, boil 2 glasses of milk, a dash of salt and nutmeg.

Then, add the hot, mashed potatoes to the boiling milk and stir with care. Add some milk or cream if the mix is too thick. Turn off heat when the mix achieves the right consistency. Blend 100 g of butter off the heat and allow to melt.

A richer variant includes adding 1 yolk and grated parmesan cheese.

This side dish is usually served with mixed boiled meat, but can be used to side other second courses.

Potato roll ✳ ✳

Ingredients and quantities for 6 people:

200 g flour
1 kg boiled potatoes
2 eggs
salt as needed
pepper as needed
nutmeg as needed

for the filling:
800 g zucchini
50 g butter
salt and pepper as needed

Mash 1 kg of hot, freshly boiled potatoes, and prepare the mix with 200 g of flour, 2 eggs, salt, pepper and nutmeg.

After blending the ingredients with care, use a tablespoon to lay the mix on a damp cloth with the aid of a rolling pin. Sprinkle with grated parmesan cheese and season with 800 g of sauté *zucchini* adding a knob of butter, or with a *trevigiano* and pineseed sauce or a *porcini* sauce or even a spinach sauce as described in the following paragraph.

Roll the cloth and cook in salted boiling water for 20-25 minutes. When lukewarm, remove the cloth. Allow to cool and then wrap with tin foil.

Cut into 1 or 2 cm thick slices. Grease a baking dish with butter and lay the slices on it, topping with butter flakes and grated parmesan cheese. Bake gratin and serve.

a) Radicchio and pine-nuts filling

Ingredients:

40 g flour
500 g julienned radicchio
2 tablespoons of olive oil
1 tablespoon chopped parsley
1 glass of red wine
30 g pine-nuts
50 g butter
garlic, rosemary, sage, salt and pepper as needed

Heat 2 tablespoons of olive oil in a frying pan. When the oil is hot, add the julienned *radicchio* and stir fry for a few minutes. Sprinkle with 1 tablespoon of chopped parsley before turning off heat. Put the *radicchio* in a bowl.

Separately, prepare a sauce with 50 g of butter and 40 g of flour. Melt the butter and brown the flour. Add 1 glass of red wine, adjust salt and pepper and add the sauce to the *radicchio*. Enrich with 30 g of pine-nuts and fill the roll.

b) Porcini mushrooms filling

Ingredients:

400 g mushrooms
50 g butter
1 garlic clove
salt and pepper as needed

It's a white sauce made with porcini mushrooms. Clean 400 g of porcini mushrooms and slice them. Stir fry them in a frying pan with 50 g of butter and season with 1 garlic clove, which will be removed at the end. Adjust salt and pepper. When the mushrooms are cooked, fill the roll.

c) Spinach filling

Ingredients:

700-800 g spinach
50 g butter
liquid cream as needed
salt as needed
nutmeg as needed

Clean 700-800 g of spinach, keeping just the leaves.

Melt 50 g of butter and plunge the spinach leaves without drying them. Sauté and adjust salt and nutmeg. Cover with a lid and allow to cook, adding a little liquid cream if necessary.

Fill the roll as described in the recipe.

Eggs with spinach ✳

Ingredients and quantities for 6 people:

1 kg spinach
100 g butter
6 eggs
50 g of grated parmesan cheese
1/2 glass of fresh, liquid cream
salt as needed
nutmeg as needed

This is not simply a side dish, but a tasty second course.

Clean 1 kg of spinach, keeping just the leaves. Melt 100 g of butter in a deep pan. When the butter is melted, add the spinach without drying them. Adjust salt and nutmeg and cover with a lid.

Use a fork to make holes in the spinach: break the 6 eggs into these holes.

Sprinkle with abundant parmesan cheese and a dash of salt. Cover again and allow to cook for 4-5 minutes.

While cooking, add some tablespoons of fresh, liquid cream on spinach in case they are too dry.

Stewed eggs ✳

Ingredients and quantities for 6 people:

6 eggs
4 garlic cloves
1 large bunch of parsley
2 tablespoons seed oil
350 g of tomato purée
salt as needed
pepper as needed

Chop 4 garlic cloves, a large bunch of parsley and stir fry in seed oil. Add 350 g of tomato purée and adjust salt and pepper. Leave on a medium-high heat.

After about 10 minutes, and only when boiling,

break the 6 eggs in the sauce. Cover with care and cook for 4 minutes more.

The stewed eggs are served as a second course, but the sauce can be used to season potato *gnocchi* and *strozzapreti*.

Fish-based second courses

Bologna does not have a great tradition about fish, except for eel, which is a typical Christmas dish, coming from the Comacchio area (in the province of Ferrara) and preferably stewed.

Or dried salt cod typically cooked in milk and herring, also known as *saracca*, which can be matched with *polenta* or bread. Now they are both out of fashion. We will pay special attention to tuna-loaf, a very appreciated dish today because it is easy to prepare for buffet meals, both formal and casual.

Stewed eel ✳ ✳

Ingredients and quantities for 6 people:
1/2 tablespoon of flour
1.2 kg eel
1/2 glass of seed oil
1 small onion
2 garlic cloves
1 tablespoon of tomato paste
parsley as needed
rosemary as needed
salt as needed
pepper as needed
red wine (as desired)

Freshly fished eel can be stored for a long time, while its flesh deteriorates quickly once the fish is dead. Therefore, it is advisable to kill it right before using it or ask the fishmonger to gut it for you if you want to use it immediately. You have to remove the head, the guts and the final part of the tail; skin it and dice it into 7-10 cm bits. Coat them with flour one by one and stir fry in oil until they are crusty.

You can also spray with a little red wine, which helps smoothing the strong taste of the river eel.

Meanwhile, prepare a base with 1 small onion, 2 garlic cloves, parsley and 1 tablespoon of seed oil. Allow to brown and add 1 tablespoon of tomato paste, diluted with water. When it starts boiling again, add the eel dice with some leaves of rosemary. Allow to cook for 15 minutes. Finally adjust salt and pepper.

The typical product of the Park

Comacchio eel

It's a snake-like fish which leaves the marshes of Comacchio and their fresh waters in order to migrate to the Sargasso Sea and there reproduce. During such crossing, fishermen catch the eel thanks to special traps called *lavorieri*.

As long ago as in the XVIII century, labs and factories used to marinate it, since it's the only way to preserve it: a tradition which gradually disappeared and which was only recently revived. In the Regional Parc of the Po Delta you can still buy fresh or even wild eel.

141

Herring in oil or "gracious" herring ✳

Ingredients and quantities for 6 people:

300 g herring
1 tablespoon of vinegar
3 tablespoon of oil for seasoning

Soak the herring the night before cooking, leaving a little water running so that the water changes automatically.

Remove the herring from the water, dry it and season it with 3 tablespoon of oil and vinegar. Allow to marinate a little, until the sauce is created. Serve with bread or *polenta*.

Dried salt cod with milk ✳

Ingredients and quantities for 6 people:

1.5 kg of fresh salt cod or 800 g of dried salt cod
flour as needed
1 glass of seed oil
milk as needed
salt and pepper as needed

Choose a white flesh fish: if it's fresh, buy at least 1.5 kg. If dried, 800 g will do. The latter should be soaked in abundant water for three days, changing the water 3 times a day. Then dry it and dice it in 5-7 cm cubes. Coat in flour firstly and then stir fry in very hot oil.

The put the bits on a baking dish and add as much milk as needed to cover them. Bake at 180° for 15 minutes.

Adjust salt before serving if necessary.

Tuna loaf ✳

Ingredients and quantities for 4 people:

2 eggs
500 g of potatoes
180 g of tuna
1 level tablespoon of capers
1 dash of anchovy paste or 1 anchovy
salt as needed
pepper as needed

Boil 500 g of potatoes, peel them and blend them with 180 g of tuna, along with its oil, 2 eggs, 1 level tablespoon of capers, a dash of anchovy paste or 1 anchovy, salt and pepper. Blend into a single mixture.

Meanwhile, grease a mould with butter (the same as the one used for *creme caramel*) and fill with the mixture. Bake, covering with tin foil, for 20 minutes. Remove the loaf from the oven and allow to cool.

Then slice it, lay the slices on a serving dish and top with mayonnaise.

The tuna loaf can be prepared the day before serving and stored in the fridge.

Don't forget...

"Artistic" tuna loaf
You can use creative moulds to shape the tuna loaf in special ways.
Serve on platters, sided by appropriate dippings and mayonnaise. It's an artistic way to decorate a buffet.

Cheese

We can say the same thing about cheese as for bread: nobody does it at home nowadays…

Some people think it's too difficult, some others refuse to practice this art, which once enabled to have a real meal based on cheese, sided by some bread or *polenta*.

Our aim is to debunk a belief of our times. Making cheese in your own kitchen is not as difficult as it may seem! It takes slightly more than 1 hour and, if eaten fresh, it can be eaten straight away. Mature cheese, on the other hand, needs to rest in a cellar before eating.

This chapter will teach you how to use your creativity to flavor cheese and will give you instructions on how to dose green pepper, mint, chili pepper, oregano and fennel. You will also learn how to make *ricotta*, a fundamental ingredient in Bolognese cooking, the lead character of fillings for many pasta dishes, mixtures and traditional sweet fillings.

Soft cheese ✲

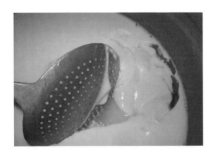

> **Ingredients and quantities for a whole piece of cheese:**
>
> 3 l milk
> 1 tablespoon rennet
> 1 large dash of salt

To make a whole cheese (buy the appropriate plastic mould with holes in specialized hardware shops), firstly pour 3 l of fresh, whole milk in a deep pan and heat until warm.

Add a little salt and cook milk until it reaches a temperature of 37°-38°. At this point, add 1 small tablespoon of rennet (you can buy it in specialized shops or at the chemist's) and stir slowly. Leave the aluminum flake soaked in the milk. Cover the pan and allow to cool for around 1 hour. Then, use the aluminum flake to break the thick cheese and whey concentrate; use the flake to rise the cheese only, separating the lumps of cheese from the whey, and put it back in the mould.

Drain the whey, shaking the mould, before leaving the cheese to rest at room temperature.

After about 1 hour, serve the fresh cheese cut into segments.

According to taste, the cheese can also be flavored with fresh herbs and spices. Before putting the lumps back in the mould, add the desired quantity of green pepper, mint, chili pepper, oregano or fennel and blend with the cheese evenly.

Mature cheese ✳ ✳

> **Ingredients and quantities for a whole piece of cheese:**
>
> 6 l milk, 2 tablespoons of rennet
> salt as needed

The process is the same as for soft cheese, although it requires the double amount of ingredients on account of the different boiling time and the maturing process.

Heat 6 l of milk in a pan, until it reaches a temperature of about 38°. Remove from heat and add 2 tablespoons of rennet (which can be found in chemists and specialized shops).

As soon as the milk lumps, boil 1 l of water and pour it in the pan. This way you will get the lumps to be broken with the aluminum flake and then stir with care. Put the pan back on heat and cook until it reaches a temperature of about 40°. At this point, compress the lumps, separating them from the whey and squeezing them with care, and put them back in the mould (the appropriate plastic mould with holes can be found in specialized hardware shops). Meanwhile, bring the whey back to boil and then turn off. Then plunge the mould and leave to cool until the next day.

Remove the mould from the whey and drain for at least 24 hours. Put it on a soup plate where it can

release some more liquid. Sprinkle 1 dash of salt up and down. Put the mould in the cellar or in another fresh place, not covering and making sure you turn it often. Leave to mature for at least 7 days.

Mature cheese can be flavored too, with spices and dry herbs, such as black and white pepper in grains and dry chili pepper.

Ricotta ✳ ✳

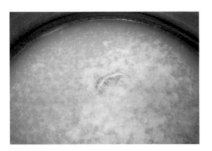

> **Approximate quantity for using the remaining whey from the making of a mature cheese:**
>
> 1 l milk
> 1 tablespoon vinegar
> 1 dash of salt
> whey remaining from making cheese

Put the whey back on heat and allow to simmer. Before it starts boiling again, add 1 l of milk, 1 tablespoon of vinegar and a dash of salt. However, remember that the original recipe does not include the addiction of milk. Today it is important because the whey does not have the same properties as the milk of the farmers of the old days.

Then, stir with the aluminum flake and turn off heat. Use a skimmer to collect the *ricotta* in the basket and strain. Allow to cool and put in the fridge.

From a hearty tradition

The *Ferragosto* holiday (15th August) was usually spent outdoors, like a real feast, with many relatives and friends. The typical dishes were gratin *cannelloni*, fried *crescentine* with Parma ham and fresh *ricotta* sided by jam of the fruit in season.
Then, everybody gathered around the barbecue to grill the meat.

Spoon desserts

There are many spoon desserts in the Bolognese tradition and they are very tasty as well: *zuppa inglese* (similar to English trifle), which is not English at all; *fior di latte*, which is often mistaken for the more famous *creme caramel*; *mascarpone*, which is always present on the tables of those who love sweets. The list includes also tasty coffee or chocolate puddings as well as the recent vanilla or strawberry Bavarian cream. Furthermore, three-colored chocolate mousse, cooked cream and walnut soufflé. Then many filled creams and *zabaglione* and chocolate chantilly cream. However, we should not forget the more common sherbets, *granitas,* and the traditional ice-creams.

Strawberry Bavarian cream ✳ ✳

Ingredients and quantities for 6-8 people:

500 g strawberries
250 g sugar
3/4 l cream
15 g isinglass
1 lemon

Make an infusion with 500 g of strawberries, 250 g of sugar and the juice of 1 lemon for about an hour. Process with a blender and sift.

Whip 3/4 l of cream until stiff and set 1 tablespoon aside. Blend softly with the sifted mix.

Melt 15 g of isinglass with the tablespoon of liquid cream previously set aside on a very low heat and add to the rest. Put in the serving bowls and then in the fridge to solidify. Serve after a few hours.

Vanilla Bavarian cream ✳ ✳

Ingredients and quantities for 6-8 people:

0.5 l milk
0,5 l cream
150 g sugar

The typical product of the Park

La pesca regina of Londa
The *pesca regina di Londa* (named after the area and the name of the man who discovered it during the 50s, Alfredo Leoni di Londa) has white flesh and red streaks near the pit: it's very sweet and perfumed.
It's a big fruit (300-400 g) and ripens late: during the second ten days of September and you can buy it only during this month and October.
It is better to enjoy it when fresh and it is a pity to put it in syrup or to make a jam out of it. The Bavarian cream with *pesca regina* is exquisite.

20 g isinglass
6 yolks
1 vanilla stick

Boil 0.5 l of milk with 1 stick of vanilla (broken). Meanwhile, soak the isinglass in water. Melt 150 g of sugar with 6 yolks. Cook on heat until it sticks to the tablespoon. Then add the isinglass after squeezing it. Sift and then whip 0.5 l of cream until stiff.

Allow to cool and then blend it with the whipped cream. Allow to solidify in the fridge for at least 4 hours before serving.

Coffee pudding *

Ingredients and quantities for 6-8 people:

0.5 l milk
100 g coffee beans
150 g sugar
2 eggs
3 yolks
salt as needed
whipped cream as desired

Bring 0.5 l of milk to boil. In the meantime, bake 100 g of coffee beans at 180°-200°. As soon as the milk starts boiling, remove from the heat and then plunge the coffee beans and allow to cool.

Put 2 whole eggs, 3 yolks, 1 dash of salt and 150 g of sugar in a separate bowl and blend with care. Then add the sifted milk, while stirring continuously.

Pour the mixture in a caramelized mould, possibly an earthenware one: it will look better on the table as you won't need to turn it upside down.

Cook in a bain-marie in a pre-heated oven (120°) for 40 minutes.

Allow to cool and decorate with whipped cream and some coffee beans.

Chocolate pudding ✳

Ingredients and quantities for 6-8 people:

90 g flour
1 l milk
100 g dark chocolate
250 g sugar
6 eggs
100 g sugar for caramel
1 dash of salt

Don't forget...

The secret for a good sweet
It may look weird and absurd but, in order to have a perfect sweet, it is always necessary to add 1 dash of salt.
This rule applies to any kind of sweet, from cakes to puddings.

Melt 100 g of dark chocolate in 1 l of milk on heat. Blend 250 g of sugar with 1 dash of salt and 90 g of flour in a bowl. Add this mixture to the hot milk and chocolate, keeping on heat until creamy.

Remove from heat, add 6 eggs and blend with care. Fill a mould, previously caramelized (see box, page 150) and cook in a bain-marie. The pudding is ready when it swells.

Allow to cool and turn the pudding upside down on a serving dish.

Italian custard ✳

Ingredients and quantities for 6-8 people:

45 g flour
125 g sugar
0.5 l milk
grated lemon peel
3 eggs
1 dash of salt

Boil 0.5 l of milk with the grated lemon peel. Meanwhile, mix 125 g of sugar, 3 eggs, 45 g of flour and 1 dash of salt in a bowl. Add the flavored, hot milk, stirring continuously. Sift and put back on heat. Blend and allow to cook until it reaches the right consistency.

Italian custard can be used to enrich cakes and tarts, or to fill cream puffs, croissants and *cannolo*. It is also the base for the *chanilly*, which decorates many cakes.

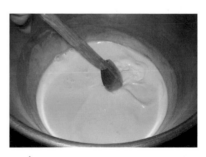

↑↓ Veil of the tablespoon.

149

English custard ✳

Ingredients and quantities for 6 people:
2 dl milk 4 yolks 70 g sugar 1 tip of vanilla stick 1 dash of vanillin

Boil 2 dl of milk with the tip of a stick of vanilla and 1 dash of vanillin. Whip 4 yolks with 70 g of sugar and add the milk (after removing the vanilla and sifting).

Put back on heat, stirring continuously.

Cook until the cream sticks to the tablespoon leaving a veil on it; allow to cool and put in the fridge. Serve after a few hours and don't store for long.

English custard can be served on ice-cream, on chocolate cakes, or on yogurt cakes. It can be matched with soft fruit salads, blackcurrants and raspberries.

Crème caramel ✳

Ingredients and quantities for 6-8 people:
7.5 l milk 175 g sugar 50 g sugar for caramel 8 eggs 1 stick of vanilla

Boil 1.5 l of milk with the broken stick of vanilla for at least 1 hour. Mix 5 eggs with 350 g of sugar and the milk. Caramelize the mould or the small moulds (see box on page 150) and fill with the mixture resulting from the above-mentioned process. Cook in a bain-marie in an oven at 130° for about 40 minutes. Allow to cool and put in the fridge. Serve cold, turning the crème caramel upside down on a serving dish.

Vanilla ice-cream ✳

Ingredients and quantities for 6-8 people:

0.5 l liquid fresh cream
0.5 l milk
250 g sugar
8 yolks
2 egg-whites
1 lemon peel
1 dash of salt

Don't forget...

Every time yolks and egg-whites are whipped separately, it is important that they don't get mixed.
Separate the yolks from the whites very carefully: don't leave a drop of white in the yolk and vice versa otherwise you won't be able to whip them properly and you will risk compromising the final result.

Boil 0.5 l of milk and 0.5 l of liquid fresh cream, together with the yellow part of a lemon's peel. Simmer for 5 minutes. Turn off heat and allow to cool down for 2 hours.

Mix 250 g of sugar, 8 yolks and 1 dash of salt. Melt with care, add milk and cream and then sift. Allow to thicken on heat, without boiling. The cream is ready when it sticks to the tablespoon, leaving a veil on it.

At this point, remove from heat and put the bottom of the pan into cold water to stop cooking.

Then pour the cream in a freezer-ware and freeze, stirring every now and then.

In order to make the ice-cream softer, add 2 whipped egg-whites before freezing. Stir softly from top to bottom and freeze.

Chocolate ice-cream ✳

Ingredients and quantities for 6-8 people:

0.5 l liquid fresh cream
0.5 l milk
200 g dark chocolate
250 g sugar
8 yolks
2 egg-whites
1 dash of salt

Follow the same process as the previous recipe. Just replace the lemon's peel with 200 g of grated dark chocolate, to be added to 0.5 l of liquid fresh cream and a 0.5 l of milk.

Then pour the cream in a freezer-ware and freeze, stirring every now and then.

In order to make the ice-cream softer, add 2 whipped egg-whites before freezing. Stir softly from top to bottom and freeze.

Fior di latte ✳

Ingredients and quantities for 6 people:

1 l milk
1 tablespoon of coffee beans
250 g sugar
6 eggs
100 g sugar for caramel
1 dash of salt

Boil 1 l of milk with 1 tablespoon of coffee beans. Allow to simmer until the milk shrinks to 1/5 of its volume. Allow to cool.

Prepare a separate bowl with 250 g of sugar, 6 eggs and 1 dash of salt. Mix the sugar and eggs with care and then add the milk, little by little. After that, sift and pour in a caramelized mould (see box p. 150).

Cook in a bain-marie in an oven for 40-45 minutes. Finally, allow to cool and put the *Fior di latte* in the fridge. Serve cold, after turning it upside down on a serving dish.

Granita ✳

Ingredients and quantities for 6-8 people:

for the syrup:
740 g water
480 g sugar

for the granita:
280 g of sifted lemon juice

Prepare the syrup putting the water and the sug-

152

ar on heat. Allow to simmer for about 10 minutes, until the liquid becomes thicker. The syrup can also be prepared and stored, in order to have it always available in the fridge.

Squash 280 g of lemon juice, sift and add it to the syrup. Stir every now and then while freezing, until it becomes a thick cream.

Mascarpone ✳ ✳

Ingredients and quantities for 6 people:

500 g mascarpone cheese
2 eggs
100 g sugar
100 g icing or vanilla sugar
1 dash of salt

Separate the yolks from the egg-whites and put in separate bowls.

Add 100 g of icing or vanilla sugar to the egg-whites (if you are using coffee-flavored *mascarpone*, it is better to use icing sugar); whip until stiff, with 1 dash of salt; add 250 g of *mascarpone* cheese and keep whipping. Put in the fridge.

Add 100 g of sugar to the yolks. Whip the ingredients together (this will take some time because the sugar needs to melt) and add 250 g of *mascarpone* cheese. Then whip again.

These two creams can be used to prepare different kinds of *mascarpone* that can be served as desired.

For example, you can alternate one layer of yellow cream with one of white cream, separated by slices of sponge cake or serve with macaroons, or flavored as desired.

In May, strawberries can be a perfect match for *mascarpone*: make an infusion with chopped strawberries, sugar and lemon juice. Then, arrange one layer of sponge cake, softened with the strawberries and with a layer of yellow cream, then continue with another layer of sponge cake, strawberries and a layer of white cream. You can also use another kind of fruit in the same way, or some sponge cake soaked in coffee.

Use only fresh *mascarpone* cheese for the best final result!

Chocolate mousse ✻ ✻

Ingredients and quantities for 6 people:

250 g dark chocolate
3 eggs
0.5 l cream
1 dash of salt

Melt 250 g of dark chocolate in a bain-marie.

Whip 3 egg-whites until stiff with 1 dash of salt. Add the 3 yolks, one by one, and whip with a hand-mixer. Whip 0.5 l of cream until stiff. Add the chocolate to the eggs and then to the whipped cream, stirring softly.

The same mousse can be prepared in three colors. Just follow the same process but change the kind of chocolate: dark, milk and white.

Then, pour the three layers of dark, milk and white chocolate in a bowl. Store in the fridge for at least 8 hours before serving.

You can use a big bowl or small serving bowl, as desired. Then, in order to have a "pudding", put in the freezer for at least 2 hours. The mousse pudding, once turned upside down on the serving dish, it remains whole for just half an hour.

Pannacotta (Cooked cream) ✻

Ingredients and quantities for 6-8 people:

250 g egg-whites
200 g icing sugar
1 l cream
1 stick of vanilla
1 isinglass
a spray of maraschino
1 dash of salt

Boil 1 l of cream with the stick of vanilla, broken or cut.

Soak an isinglass for at least 10-15 minutes and then plunge it into the hot cream. Its function is to give elasticity to the mix.

Isinglass proves an effective ingredient, above all for the *pannacotta* version to be served during refreshments, prepared in one mould only.

Caramelize the mould or the small moulds (see box page 150); blend 250 g of egg-whites with 200 g of icing sugar separately, making sure they don't foam. Add the flavored cream little by little and then a spray of maraschino. Finally pass through a sift.

Fill the caramelized mould or small moulds. Cook in a bain-marie in an oven at 130°-140° for about 40-45 minutes.

Allow to cool and store in the fridge. Turn upside down on the serving dish.

The spray of maraschino can be replaced with another flavoring, giving the *pannacotta* the desired taste: coffee, anise, cinnamon, vanilla and more.

Chocolate sauce ✳

Ingredients and quantities for 6-8 people:

2.5 dl cream
1.2 ml milk
60 g sugar
20 g cocoa
50 g dark chocolate
1 teaspoon of starch
1 dash of vanillin

Mix 2.5 dl cream, 1.2 ml of milk, 60 g of sugar, 20 g of cocoa, 1 teaspoon of starch, 50 g of dark chocolate and 1 dash of vanillin and cook in a bain-marie until creamy for about 30 minutes.

Serve the chocolate sauce still hot in serving bowls or use it as a topping for cakes and meringues.

Sherbet ✳ ✳

Ingredients and quantities for 6-8 people:

for the syrup:
2 l water
1 kg sugar

for the strawberry sherbet:
500 g strawberry
juice of 1/2 lemon
3 egg-whites
1 dash of salt

for the mint sherbet:
500 g mint syrup
chopped fresh mint leaves
3 egg-whites
1 dash of salt

The basic syrup for the sherbet is prepared with 2 l of water and 1 kg of sugar. It can be prepared and stored. Boil the water with the sugar for 5-10 minutes, allowing to foam. Cool, then sift and store in a bottle in the fridge.

For the strawberry sherbet: make an infusion with 500 g of strawberries, diced, and the juice of 1/2 lemon. Leave to macerate for 2 hours at room temperature. Blend with a hand mixer. Put the resulting mix in a bowl with as much sugar syrup (check proportions with a measured jug). Stir with care.

Separately, whip 3 egg-whites until stiff with 1 dash of salt and add to the syrup, stirring from top to bottom. Store in the freezer. As it solidifies on the surface, stir the sherbet. Eat straight away when ready. Do not store.

For the mint sherbet: follow the same process but, instead of strawberries, add the same quantity of mint syrup. Before serving, decorate with some chopped fresh mint leaves.

Walnut soufflé ✳ ✳

Ingredients and quantities for 6 people:

1 tablespoon of flour
3 yolks
35 g icing sugar
70 g butter
70 g ground walnuts
3 egg-whites
80 g icing sugar
75 g dark chocolate
1 dash of salt

Whip 3 yolks with 35 g of icing sugar, 70 g of soft butter and 1 dash of salt. Then, add 1 tablespoon of flour and 70 g of ground walnuts and stir.

Melt 75 g of dark chocolate in a bain-marie. Make it lukewarm and then add it to the mix.

Whip 3 egg-whites until stiff and softly stir from top to bottom.

Grease the moulds with butter and dust with icing sugar. Fill them and cook in a bain-marie in an oven at 160° for 20-30 minutes.

Serve the walnut soufflé hot, sided by English custard.

Tiramisù ✳ ✳

Ingredients and quantities for 6-8 people:

1 kg mascarpone
4 eggs
200 g sugar
200 g icing or vanilla sugar
1/2 glass of coffee
6-8 biscuits, macaroon-like

Mix the two *mascarpone* creams (see *mascarpone* recipe, page 153), the white one and the yellow one. Whip them together and add 1/2 glass of coffee. Prepare the serving boils with crumbled macaroons on the bottom.

Finally, dust with bitter cocoa powder.

Whipped zabaglione ✳

↑ Veiling of the whip.

Ingredients and quantities for 1 person:
1 yolk
half egg-shell of marsala liquor
half egg-shell of sugar

Use 1 yolk per person. Add a half egg-shell full of *marsala* and half egg-shell of sugar. Blend together and, while whipping, cook in a bain-marie. The *zabaglione* is ready when it sticks to the whisk.

The whipped *zabaglione* can be served hot in serving bowls, sided by some biscuits.

Zuppa inglese (English trifle) ✳

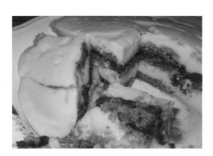

Ingredients and quantities for 6-8 people:
For the cream:
60 g flour
3/4 l milk
200 g sugar
6 yolks
75 g of dark chocolate
a spray of alchermes
sponge cake
a lemon's peel
1 dash of salt

Heat 3/4 l of milk with the yellow part of the lemon's peel.

Mix 6 yolks, 200 of sugar and 1 dash of salt in a separate bowl until creamy. Add 60 g of flour, stir again and add the lukewarm milk.

Pass through a sift and put back on heat, stirring continuously. Cook the yellow cream and, when it starts boiling, leave on heat for one more minute and then turn off. Keep stirring for at least 5 minutes.

Meanwhile, line a bowl with the sliced sponge cake, slightly wet with alchermes. Keep 3 tablespoons of yellow cream aside and add 75 g of dark chocolate; cook in a bain-marie until the chocolate melts and becomes creamy.

At this point, put a layer of hot yellow cream in the bowl, a slice of sponge cake wet with alchermes and a layer of chocolate cream, then another slice of sponge cake and then yellow cream again. You can put the first layer of sponge cake in one direction and the second one in another direction. Serve with the bowl.

Cakes

There are many old recipes that have been handed down over the years. There are also many modern variants, which include new ingredients. Each holiday in Bologna has its cake: the *certosino* or *pan speziale* for Christmas, the *ciambella* for Easter, the *torta degli addobbi*, also known as "rice cake", which is offered to relatives and friends during the various parish feasts in town. Moreover, there is a traditional cake, that is the *tagliatelle* cake, which has always been an icon because it succeeds in combining short-crust and sweet *taglioline* pastry.

The best way to have breakfast is with a slice of *torta margherita* (sponge cake), or *brazadèla*, soaked in latte. Apple pie is another cake that is very appreciated for snacks, even better if dusted with icing sugar.

For children, and for adults, the Nutella and cream cake or the lovely chocolate cake and many fruit tarts. And also meringue, which can be considered the formal cake for Communion, confirmation and weddings.

This chapter will also illustrate some famous recipes, such as *montebianco* and the *Saint Honoré*, to stimulate everybody to make homemade cakes.

Certosino or pan speziale ✳ ✳

Quantities for 6 certosini:

1.8 kg flour
1 kg candied orange
700 g almonds
700 g fruit pickles
500 g candied citron
350 g sugar
200 g honey
100 g dark chocolate
80 g pine-nuts
80 g bitter cocoa
0.75 g ammonia
0.75 g spices (cinnamon, cloves, laurel, lemon and orange peel)
laurel wine as needed

for the decoration:
candied fruit as desired
honey for brushing

This is the Christmas cake, which is traditionally made and given to friends and relatives. People usually don't do just one at a time because its making is long and laborious.

Mix 1.8 kg of flour with laurel wine, as much as needed to blend all the ingredients, gradually adding 350 g of sugar, 700 g of almonds, 700 g of fruit pickles, 200 g of honey (heated with 100 g of dark chocolate), 80 g of pine-nuts, 80 g of bitter cocoa, 0.75 g of ammonia and 0.75 g of spices: cinnamon, cloves, lemon or orange peel.

Work the dough with energy, continuously adjusting with laurel wine.

Make strips of dough and join the two ends, making small rings with a hole in the middle that will close during cooking. Fill and decorate with 1 kg of candied orange, 500 g candied citron and some candied cherries. Bake at 160° for 15-20 minutes.

Leave to rest and cool on a board for at least 20 days, during which, every 2 days, the surface of every piece must be brushed with honey as soon as they dry.

Thus the *certosino* gets dry but not stale.

Finally, wrap them in plastic wrap and close with a red ribbon. The presents are ready.

From a hearty tradition

The *certosino* or *pan speziale* was usually eaten at Christmas Eve. It was never the *certosino* made at home, because that was given to relatives and friends. So people ate the one that friends had given them. The *pan speziale* had a precise meaning: it represented the result of a year's work and was the cake of the family. Almost all the ingredients, in fact, can be found at home: fruit pickles, dry fruit, candied fruit, and even laurel or juniper wine.

Easter Ciambella ✳

Ingredients and quantities for 2 ciambelle:

500 g flour
3 eggs
200 g sugar
100 g butter
1 sachet of chemical yeast
milk for brushing
grains of sugar and powdered sugar
grated peel of 1 lemon

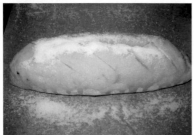

Heat 1 glass of milk with 100 g of butter until warm.

Knead on a board or in a wide bowl 3 eggs, a little grated lemon peel, 1 sachet of yeast, 1 dash of salt and 500 g of flour. Add milk with the melted butter and knead all the ingredients together, firstly with the tablespoon and then with your hands.

To complete the Easter *ciambella,* lay the dough on greaseproof paper and make some transversal cuts. Brush the surface with milk with abundant powdered sugar and some grain of sugar.

Bake at 160° for about 50 minutes.

Ciambella or brazadèla ✳

Ingredients and quantities for 1 ciambella:

350 g flour
100 g sugar
60 g o butter
10 g of chemical yeast
1 egg
milk as needed, grated peel of 1 lemon
milk for brush

The *brazadèla* is similar to the Easter *ciambella,* at least for the preparation process, but the proportion of sugar, butter and flour and the quantity of the grated peel of a lemon vary.

Heat 1 glass of milk with 60 g of butter; melt and allow to cool.

Knead on a board or in a wide bowl 350 g of flour, 1 egg, the grated peel of 1 lemon, 10 g of chemical yeast and 100 g of sugar. Add the lukewarm milk with butter and knead all the ingredients together, firstly with a tablespoon and then with your hands.

Shape the dough, brush the surface with milk and bake at 160° for 50 minutes.

The same dough can be used to make delicious jam or chocolate tarts.

Don't forget...

The ciambella with jam
Lay the *ciambella* or *brazadèla* dough with a thickness of 1.5 cm and spread apricot, strawberry, blackcurrants jam or any other homemade jam on it (except for fruit pickles, which is usually used to fill the *pinza,* page 167).
Roll as a strudel and then make a *ciambella* roll. Brush with a little milk and dust with powdered sugar, adding some bigger grain of sugar.
Bake at 160° for 50 minutes.

Apple and nut ciambella ✳ ✳ ✳

Ingredients and quantities for 1 ciambella (pie dish with a diameter of 30 cm):

200 g flour
150 g margarine
225 g sugar
75 g ground hazelnuts
50 g whole hazelnuts
1 peeled and ground apple
1 egg
1 yolk
milk as needed
1 dash of bicarb
1 dash of salt

Whisk 150 g of margarine and 225 g of sugar. Add 1 whole egg and 1 yolk.

Mix 200 g of sifted flour with 1 dash of salt and 1 dash of bicarb.

Then, add 75 g of ground hazelnuts, 50 g of whole hazelnuts, 1 peeled and ground apple; finally, blend adding as many tablespoons of milk as needed.

Pour the mix in the holed mould, filling only halfway through. Bake at 160° for 40-45 minutes.

Allow to cool and rest until the next day. The apple and hazelnut *ciambella* can be put on the serving dish only if cold, otherwise it could break.

The typical product of the Park

Honey
All the villages in the National Park of *Foreste casentinesi*, *Monte Falterona*, *Campigna* produce very good honey. There are many varieties of it, with different colors and tastes, depending mainly on the different flowers and climate.

Honey features simple sugars, vitamins, enzymes and mineral salts.

The market offers a wide range of it the whole year through: acacia, millefiori, *medica*, *sulla*, lime, chestnut, forest honeydew and fir honeydew. Choose the desired type of honey for the Bolognese recipes of Christmas *panone* and *certosino*.

Ricotta and fruit tart ✳

Ingredients and quantities for 4 people (pie dish with a diameter of 30 cm):

For the short crust:
200 g flour
80 g sugar
80 g butter
1 egg
yeast

per il ripieno:
175 g of sugar
500 g of ricotta

4 eggs
50 g starch
mixed fruit
1/2 sachet of yeast for cakes
grated peel of 1 lemon
vanillin or lemon
1 dash of salt
apricot jelly

Prepare the short crust with 200 g of flour, 80 g of sugar, 80 g of butter, 1/2 sachet of yeast for cakes, the grated peel of 1 lemon and 1 dash of salt.

Crumble the ingredients with your hands, make a well with 1 egg in the middle and knead quickly. Lay the short crust and fill the pie dish, adhering to the sides well.

Blend 4 eggs, 175 g of sugar, 500 g of *ricotta*, 50 g of starch, 1 dash of vanillin or 1 lemon peel and a little salt. Blend the mix with care and spread it on the short crust.

Decorate with well diced fruit in season and bake at 160° for 35-40 minutes.

Finally, coat the surface with apricot jelly. Put in the fridge at least 1 hour before serving.

Fruit can be replaced with pine-nuts if preferred, sprinkling them on the top layer of ricotta fill. Dust with vanilla sugar after baking. This version is commonly known as *torta della nonna* (granny's cake).

Two-color ciambella ✻

Ingredients and quantities for 6 people (pie dish with a diameter of 30 cm):

350 g flour
4 eggs
200 g sugar
100 g butter
1 sachet of yeast
1 tablespoon of milk
1 tablespoon of Nutella
grated peel of 1 lemon

Pass 350 g of flour through a sift with 1 sachet of yeast. Melt 100 g of butter in a bain-marie.

Blend 4 eggs with 200 g of sugar and add 350 g of flour together with the sachet of yeast, the grated peel of 1 lemon and, finally, 100 g of melted butter. Slowly add 1 tablespoon of milk as well.

Knead all the ingredients and split the dough, setting 2/3 aside and keeping 1/3. Add 1 tablespoon of Nutella to the latter third.

Put the chocolate part on the remaining 2/3, previously poured in the buttered and floured mould, and flatten with a palette.

Bake at 160° for 40 minutes.

Meringue ✳ ✳

Ingredients and quantities for 6-8 people:
300 g egg-white
500 g of sugar
50 g of vanilla sugar
yolks
sugar
marsala
1 l cream
Black cherries in syrup
grains of chocolate
1 dash of salt

First of all, weight 300 g of egg-whites and keep the yolks aside.

Whisk the egg-whites with 1 dash of salt, 500 g of sugar and 50 g of vanilla sugar until you get a shiny foam. This process takes a little time.

Use a pastry bag to mould on greaseproof paper two dishes that will be used as bases for the cake and to make some *spumone*. Bake at 60° for at least 4 hours.

Whisk the yolks in a bain-marie in a separate pan, after weighing them, adding the same quantity of *marsala* and sugar. Let the *zabaglione* cool.

Whisk the same amount of cream (the same as yolks, sugar and *marsala*) and add it to the *zabaglione*, stirring: thus you get a *zabaglione chantilly*. At this point, lay a meringue dish on a serving dish and season with the *zabaglione chantilly*, some grains of chocolate and overlap the other dish. Cover

with whipped cream and decorate as desired with black cherries in syrup along the border, alternating them with *spumoni* or sugared almonds.

Meringue is usually the cake for baptisms, Communions, confirmations and weddings. It's always there in special events.

Montebianco ✳

Ingredients and quantities for 6-8 people:
600 g boiled and peeled chestnuts 3 dl cream 100 g mascarpone 100 g icing sugar 1 tablespoon of icing sugar for the cream 1 sachet of vanillin 1 tablespoon of amaretto 1 tablespoon of brandy 1 dash of salt lemon peel

Boil 600 g of peeled chestnuts in a little water with the lemon peel and 1 dash of salt and sugar. Process them with a vegetable mill and add 100 g of *mascarpone*, 100 g of icing sugar, 1 sachet of vanillin, 1 tablespoon of *amaretto* and 1 tablespoon of brandy. Mix the ingredients, press the mixture with a potato masher and compress it, shaping it like a "mountain".

Whip 3 dl of cream with 1 tablespoon of vanilla sugar and coat the "mountain" completely. Before serving, dust with bitter cocoa, with the help of a sift.

Sponge cake ✳ ✳

Ingredients and quantities for 6 people (pie dish with a diameter of 30 cm):

> 120 g flour
> 3 eggs
> 100 g sugar
> salt as needed

Process 3 eggs, 100 g of sugar and 1 dash of salt for at least 15 minutes with a hand mixer,.

Add 120 g of sifted flour slowly and stirring from the bottom to the top with a wooden tablespoon in order to avoid that the mixture goes runny.

Pour in a well-greased and floured pie dish. Bake for about 30 minutes at 160°, without opening the oven when finished cooking.

<table>
<tr><td>Don't forget...</td></tr>
<tr><td>Sponge cake can be stored in the freezer as well
It is advisable to keep a sponge cake stored in the freezer.
If you slice it, it can be used still frozen as a base to prepare English trifle or mascarpone.</td></tr>
</table>

Panone ✳ ✳

> **Ingredients and quantities for 12 people:**
>
> 750 g flour
> 150 g almond (half grounded and half whole)
> 150 g candied citron
> 100 g mixed candied fruit
> 50 g pine-nuts
> 100 g sultana
> 100 g peeled walnuts
> 300 g jam (fruit pickles or apricot)
> 100 g butter
> 100 g icing vanilla sugar
> 200 g sugar
> 200 g dried figs
> 50 g dark chocolate in pieces
> 50 g chocolate powder
> 1 glass of white wine
> powder yeast
> 2 eggs
> milk as needed
> candied and almond for decorating
> orange cognac
> honey for brush
> grated peel of 1 lemon

Start preparing the dough the night before. Mix 750 g of flour, 1 glass of white wine, 150 g of almonds (half ground and half whole), 150 g of candied citron, 100 g mixed candied fruit, 50 g of pine-nuts, 100 g of sultana, 100 g of peeled walnuts, 300 g of fruit pickles or apricot jam, 100 g of butter, 100 g of vanilla icing sugar, 200 g of sugar, 2 eggs, 200 g of dried figs, 50 g of dark chocolate in pieces, 50 g of chocolate powder, the grated peel of 1 lemon.

Cover the mixture, well pressed, with plastic wrap and let it rest all night at room temperature.

The next morning, add 1 sachet and a half of powder yeast, mixing it with a little milk.

Lay the dough in a baking pan. Top with almonds and candied fruit. Bake at 160° for half an hour. Finally spray with orange cognac and brush with honey.

Pinza ✳

Ingredients and quantities for a pinza:
250 g flour
100 g icing sugar
75 g margarine or butter
milk as needed
2 eggs
1 egg for brushing
200 g of fruit pickles
1/2 sachet of yeast
vanilla flavor
a sprinkling of sugar
grated peel of 1 lemon
salt as needed

Prepare the short crust making a well with 250 g of flour, 2 eggs, as much milk as needed to knead, 100 g of icing sugar, 75 g of margarine or butter (softened at room temperature), 1/2 sachet of yeast, vanilla flavor, 1 dash of salt and the grated peel of 1 lemon. Once the dough is ready, cover it and put it in the fridge for at least 30 minutes.

Roll out a square of short crust, spread the fruit pickles on it and fold it as a book, three times.

Brush with the milk and dust with sugar.

Bake at 160° for 40 minutes.

Strawberry cake ✳ ✳

**gredients and quantities for 6 people (pie dish
with a diameter of 30 cm):**

for the short crust:
400 g flour
2 eggs
160 g butter
160 g sugar
1 teaspoon of chemical yeast
1 dash of salt
grated peel of 1 lemon

for the cream:
40 g flour
0.5 l milk
1 egg
3 yolks
150 g sugar
grated peel of 1 lemon

for the filling:
2 egg-whites
50 g grated macaroons

for the decoration:
strawberries
apricot jelly

This cake is similar to a tart. The short crust must
be prepared with 400 g of flour, 160 g of butter, 160 g
of sugar, the grated peel of 1 lemon, 1 dash of salt and
1 teaspoon of chemical yeast. Mix the ingredients
and make a well with 2 eggs in the middle. Prepare
the dough and line the mould, pinching the border
with your fingers.

Firstly, prepare a cream with 0.5 l of milk, 1 egg, 3
yolks, 40 g of flour, 150 g of sugar and the grated peel
of a lemon. Then, the other filling with 2 egg-whites
whisked until stiff and 50 g of grated macaroons. Use
this latter filling to fill the pie dish. Bake for 40-45
minutes at 160°.

Finally, remove from the oven and allow to cool.
Lay on a dish and pour the cream on top. Decorate
with the strawberries, cut into halves or segments,
and coat with the apricot jelly. Put in the fridge at
least 1 hour before serving.

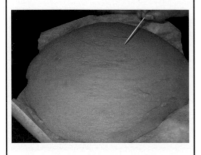

Pineapple cake * *

Ingredients and quantities for 6 people (pie dish with a diameter of 30 cm):

300 g flour
400 g sugar
300 g butter
6 eggs
1 dash of vanillin
1/2 glass of maraschino
400 g pineapple in syrup
cherries in syrup
powder yeast for 500 g of flour
100 g sugar for caramel
pineapple syrup
1 dash of salt

Melt 100 g of sugar and 2 tablespoons of water in a baking pan, rotating it in order to cover its whole surface with an even layer of caramel. Then, line the mould with the sliced pineapple. Process 300 g of butter and 400 g of sugar with a blender. Add the 6 yolks, one by one, and 1 dash of vanillin, 300 g of flour, gradually sifted, and the powder yeast.

Whisk the egg-whites until stiff; add them softly to the mixture stirring with a wooden tablespoon from the top to the bottom.

Pour in a mould and bake in a pre-heated oven at 160°, for 55 minutes without opening the oven door.

Let the cake rest in the oven for 5 minutes after turning off, then remove it from the oven and lay it on a serving dish. Spray with *maraschino* and pineapple syrup.

Finally, decorate with the cherries, putting them in the middle of each pineapple slice.

Carrot cake *

Ingredients and quantities for 6 people (pie dish with a diameter of 30 cm):

250 g flour
250 g grated carrots

170

250 g sugar
150 g ground almonds
6 eggs

Whisk 6 egg-whites until stiff with 50 g of sugar and 1 dash of salt. Then, melt 6 yolks with 200 g of sugar and add 250 g of grated carrots, 150 g of ground almonds and 250 g of sifted flour. Blend the mixture with the whisked egg-whites and stir.

Fill a buttered pie dish and bake at 160° for about 45 minutes.

Chocolate cake ✳

Ingredients and quantities for 6 people (pie dish with a diameter of 30 cm):

40 g flour
100 g sugar
125 g dark chocolate
100 g butter
4 eggs
1 dash of salt

Melt 125 g of dark chocolate in a bain-marie with 100 g of butter and 1 dash of salt; add 70 g of sugar, 3 yolks and 1 whole egg. Mix the 3 whisked egg-whites with 30 g of sugar. When the dough is ready, add 40 g of sifted flour.

Stir with a tablespoon, softly, from top to bottom. Lay the dough on a baking pan without pressing too hard.

Bake at 160° and turn off when the surface becomes crispy.

Custard cake ✳ ✳

Ingredients and quantities for 6 people (pie dish with a diameter of 30 cm):

for the short crust:
200 g flour
80 g sugar
80 g butter
1 egg
1/2 sachet of yeast for cakes
grated peel of 1 lemon
1 dash of salt

for the yellow cream:
45 g flour
3 eggs
125 g sugar
grated peel of 1 lemon
vanilla sugar

Prepare a short crust with 200 g of flour, 80 g of sugar, 80 g of butter, 1/2 sachet of yeast for cakes, the grated peel of a lemon and 1 dash of salt. Make a well with the ingredients putting 1 egg in the middle and blend. Roll it out with a rolling pin between two sheets of greaseproof paper: one part will be lain on the pie dish and the other will be used as a lid.

Meanwhile, prepare the yellow cream mixing 3 eggs, 125 g of sugar, 45 g of flour and the grated lemon peel. Boil and stir continuously. Turn off heat when the cream is thick and shiny.

After lining the pie dish with the first layer of dough, fill it with the cream and cover with the other thin layer of short crust. Bake at 160° for 30 minutes. Dust with vanilla sugar when still hot.

The custard cake can be served both hot and fridge cold.

Yogurt cake ✳

Ingredients and quantities for 6 people (pie dish with a diameter of 30 cm):

3 pot of flour

1 yogurt pot
2 pots of sugar
125 g butter
3 eggs
1 sachet of vanilla yeast for cakes

Separate the egg-whites and the yolks of 3 eggs. Whisk the egg-whites until stiff with 1 dash of salt and set aside.

Melt 125 g of butter and add a yogurt pot. Using the yogurt pot as a measurement, add 3 pots of flour, 2 pots of sugar and 1 sachet of vanilla yeast for cakes. Pour the whisked egg-whites, blend softly and stir with care. Then, fill a wide, deep baking pan (making sure the cake is 2-3 cm thick).

Bake for 45 minutes at 160°-180°. Use a toothpick to check the cooking of the central part of the cake: the cake is ready when the toothpick stays dry and the surface gets crispy.

Almond cake ✳

Ingredients and quantities for 6 people (pie dish with a diameter of 30 cm):

100 g flour
300 g ground, toasted, peeled almonds
300 g sugar
2 eggs
150 g butter
100 g crumbled macaroons
1 sachet of vanilla

Whisk 150 g of butter with 150 g of sugar and, in a separate bowl, 2 yolks with 150 g of sugar. Add the two parts and add, stirring with care, 100 g of flour, 100 g of crumbled macaroons and 300 g of almonds (peeled, toasted and ground) and 1 sachet of vanilla.

Whisk the egg-whites until stiff and softly add to the other ingredients.

Pour in a baking pan and cook for about 40 minutes at 160°.

173

Apple pie ✳ ✳

Ingredients and quantities for 6 people (pie dish with a diameter of 30 cm):

150 g flour
150 g butter (or margarine)
150 g sugar
500 g apples
4 eggs
1 sachet of vanilla
1/2 sachet of powder yeast
20 g vanilla sugar
1 dash of salt

Clean 500 g of apples and slice them finely. Whisk 4 eggs until stiff with 150 g of sugar, 1 dash of salt and 1 sachet of vanilla.

Sift 150 g of flour and 1/2 sachet of powder yeast.

Melt 150 g of butter (or margarine) in a bain-marie and allow to cool. Mix the butter with the flour and stir with care. Then, add the egg foam and 150 g of sugar. Add the apples and stir.

Pour the mixture in a baking pan, previously buttered and floured, and bake at 160° for 50 minutes.

When finished cooking, let it rest 5 minutes in the oven turned off.

Dust with vanilla sugar when still hot and then serve.

Walnut cake ✳

Ingredients and quantities for 6 people (pie dish with a diameter of 30 cm):

300 g flour
150 g finely ground walnuts
50 g of walnuts with a whole kernel for decoration
4 eggs
120 g melted butter
1 glass of milk
250 g of sugar
1 sachet of yeast
salt as needed

Melt 120 g of butter with 1 glass of milk. Whip 4 eggs with 250 g of sugar. Add 150 g of finely ground walnuts and 1 dash of salt. Mix with 300 g of sifted flour with 1 sachet of yeast.

Butter the mould, pour the dough and decorate with the kernels. Bake at 180° for about 40 minutes.

Nutella (chocolate spread) and cream cake ✳

> **Ingredients and quantities for 6-8 people (rectangular baking pan 30 x 40 cm):**
>
> 80 g flour
> 8 yolks
> 4 egg-whites
> 100 g sugar
> 20 g starch
> 25 g vanilla sugar
> 1 jar of Nutella 200 g
> whipped cream
> grated peel of a lemon
> 1 dash of salt

Whisk 8 yolks with 50 g of sugar and 25 g of vanilla sugar in a bowl until creamy; whisk the egg-whites with 50 g of sugar and a dash of salt in a separate bowl.

Mix the two creams, add the grated peel of 1 lemon, sift 80 g of flour with 20 g of starch and add slowly. Stir the mixture from top to bottom (to keep it from going runny) and pour it on greaseproof paper, making a 1 cm thick layer. Bake in a pre-heated oven at 160°-180° for 10 minutes until the cake stays soft and gets pink on the border.

Remove form the oven and turn it onto another sheet of greaseproof paper to dry the exceeding humidity.

At this point, cut it into 3 cm thick slices, top with Nutella and roll them. Make a spiral with all the slices, one after the other, until you get a single round spiral.

Lay on a serving dish and top with abundant whipped cream. Garnish and decorate as desired.

Allow to rest in the fridge for at least 45 minutes before serving. It's perfect for snacks and for children's parties.

Rice cake or torta degli addobbi ✳ ✳

Ingredients and quantities for 6 people:

1 l of milk
100 g common rice
300 g sugar
100 g ground almonds
100 g ground candied citron
50 g crumbled macaroons
1/2 glass of bitter almond liquor
5 eggs
grated peel of 1 lemon

Cook 100 g of common rice with 1 l of milk, for about 40 minutes, with 300 g of sugar and the grated peel of 1 lemon.

Then, remove from heat and add 100 g of ground almonds, 100 g of ground candied citron and 50 g crumbled macaroons. Allow to cool, stirring every now and then.

Whisk 5 eggs and add the rice. Bake at a low temperature (150°) for 1 hour and a half.

Remove from heat and spray with 1/2 glass of bitter almond liquor.

Serve the cake, cold and sliced or diced. Lay the pieces on platters with a toothpick each.

Tagliatelle cake ✳ ✳ ✳

Ingredients and quantities for 6 people (pie dish with a diameter of 30 cm):

for the short crust:
200 g flour
80 g sugar
80 g butter
1 egg
1/2 sachet of yeast for cakes
grated peel of 1 lemon and 1 dash of salt

> **for the filling:**
> 180 g sugar
> 250 g almonds
> some drops of almond flavor
>
> **for the taglioline pastry:**
> 220 g flour
> 2 eggs
> 2-3 tablespoons of brandy
> 1 butter knob

Prepare the short crust with 200 g of flour, 80 g of sugar, 80 g of butter, 1/2 sachet of yeast for cakes, the grated peel of 1 lemon and 1 dash of salt. Crumble the ingredients with your hands, make a well with 1 egg in the middle and knead quickly. Set the dough aside and then line the base and the borders of a pied dish, decorating the border with your hands.

Then, grind 250 g of almonds and mix 180 g sugar in a bowl, and some drops of almond flavor.

Fill the pie dish with this dough and lay with the *taglioline* made by kneading 220 g of flour, 2 eggs, 2-3 tablespoons of brandy and 1 butter knob. Roll out a thin pastry, allow to dry and cut the *taglioline* (note: it's not necessary to use 2 eggs of *taglioline* to make a cake; it is advisable to use less eggs, thus the remaining part can be fried in a frying pan, according to the fried *tagliatelle* recipe, see recipe page 188*).*

Finally, sprinkle with some butter flakes and dust with sugar. Bake at 150°-160° for about 40 minutes.

Dust with vanilla sugar before serving.

Torta margherita ✳

> **Ingredients and quantities for 6 people (pie dish with a diameter of 30 cm):**
>
> 150 g flour
> 225 g icing sugar
> 75 g starch
> 6 eggs

6 yolks
100 g melted butter
vanillin

Whisk 6 whole eggs and 6 yolks and 225 g of icing sugar. Add, while sifting, 150 g of flour, mixed with 75 g of starch. Add slowly 100 g of melted and cold butter and blend with care, stirring from top to bottom.

Bake at 160° for about 40 minutes.

The *torta margherita* is a simple but delicious cake. It can be filled and flavored as desired, with different creams, whipped cream and jam.

Torta sabbiosa (Sandy cake) ✳

Ingredients and quantities for 6 people (pie dish with a diameter of 30 cm):

350 g butter or margarine
300 g sugar
350 g starch
150 g flour
3 eggs
1/2 sachet of yeast
vanilla flavor
icing sugar as needed
1 dash of salt

Whisk 350 g of butter or margarine with 300 g of sugar until you get a soft mix. Add 3 yolks, 350 g of starch, 150 g of flour and 1/2 starch of sifted yeast. Add also the whisked egg-whites with 1 dash of salt and the vanilla flavor.

Butter and flour the mould, fill it halfway through and bake at 200° for about 30 minutes.

The *torta sabbiosa* is served cold, dusted with icing sugar.

Saint–Honoré cake ✳ ✳ ✳

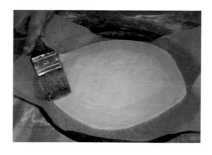

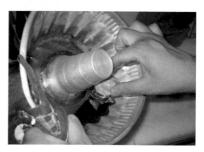

Ingredients and quantities for 6 people (pie dish with a diameter of 30 cm):

for the pâte brisée:
300 g flour
140 g butter
15 g sugar
1 dl water
1 dash of salt

for the puff pastry:
225 g flour
3 dl water
140 g butter
350 g eggs

for the chantilly cream:
25 g flour
0.25 milk
1 egg
1 yolk
80 g sugar
grated peel of 1 lemon
0.25 cream
1 dash of salt

for the zabaglione chantilly:
80 g yolks
80 g sugar
80 g marsala
0.25 cream
100 g sugar for caramel
0.25 whipped cream
1 egg for brushing

Prepare the pâte brisée mixing 300 g of flour, 140 g of butter, 15 g of sugar, 1 dash of salt and 1 dl of cold water. Process it and shape it as a dish that will be the base of the cake and pierce the bottom with a fork.

Brush the base border with the egg and, in the meantime, prepare the puff pastry (see recipe of the puff pastry on page 181) with 3 dl of water, 140 g of butter, 225 g of flour and 350 g of eggs. Use this dough to make the border and the cream puffs. Put the border made with puff pastry on the border of the base with the help of a pastry bag.

Bake at 160° for 40 minutes. Allow to cool. Meanwhile, cook the cream puffs for about 40 minutes. Fill

179

with whipped cream and attach them to the border with the caramel.

Make the chantilly cream with 1/4 g of milk, 1 whole egg, 1 yolk, 80 g of sugar, 1 dash of salt, 25 g of flour and the grated peel of 1 lemon. Whisk 1/4 of l of cream and add it to the mixture, stirring. At the same time, make the *zabaglione chantilly* mixing 80 g of yolks, 80 g of sugar, 80 g of *marsala* and adding 1/4 of l of whipped cream in the end.

Fill the cake with chantilly cream and garnish as desired with *zabaglione chantilly* puffs and whipped cream.

You can also make some chocolate *chantilly* puffs. The chocolate *chantilly* is made whisking 1 l of cream with 100 g of sugared cocoa.

Torta sbrisolona (Crumbly cake) ✳

From a hearty tradition

The recipe of the *sbrisolona* cake is very old. It could be stored in any place and for a long time in tin boxes and was always available in every house, so that it could be offered with a cup of coffee or with a glass of wine or *rosolio*.

Ingredients and quantities for 6 people (pie dish with a diameter of 30 cm):

150 g fine cornmeal
150 g starch
300 g butter
300 g sugar
4 eggs
1 tablespoon of *sassolino* (herb-based liquor), *sambuca* or anise
grated peel of 1 lemon
1/2 sachet of chemical yeast
butter and flour for the pie dish, 1 dash of salt

Whisk 300 g of butter and 300 g of sugar with a hand mixer until you get a white foam.

Add 4 yolks, one by one, making sure you don't whisk the mixture. Add slowly 150 g of fine cornmeal, 150 g of starch, 1/2 sachet of chemical yeast and the grated peel of 1 lemon. Blend 3 egg-whites with 1 dash of salt, after whisking them until stiff. Flavor with 1 tablespoon of *sassolino*, *sambuca* or anise.

Butter and flour a pie dish: fill with the mixture and bake at 160° for 40-45 minutes.

Turn off the oven and remove the pie dish only when cold.

Store in a tin box or wrapped in tin foil.

Tasty delights

This section is dedicated to tasty delights, that is all those small sweets that can enrich a platter at tea or coffee time or give a sweet ending to a fulfilling lunch.

It's difficult to say no to these tasty delights, which are served in very small portions sometimes! *Tortelloni* filled with custard and sweet *tagliatelle*, *raviole* stuffed with fruit pickles and chestnut. Finally, some advice on how to make tasty dry cookies, flavored, that can be stored to be enjoyed at any time of the day.

Cream puffs ✳ ✳ ✳

Ingredients and quantities for 6 people:

225 g flour
3 dl water
140 g butter
350 g eggs
1 dash salt

Melt 140 g of butter and 3 dl of water on heat with 1 dash of salt. When it starts boiling, add 225 g of sifted flour.

Mix with a wooden tablespoon until you get a smooth and even mixture. Keep stirring on heat until the mixture gets thicker and detaches from the borders and from the bottom of the pan, with a little frizzling, as if frying. Then, allow to cool.

Add 350 g of eggs (which are usually 7 eggs), blending with the wooden tablespoon 1 egg at a time and adding the next one only when the previous one has been completely absorbed, stirring continuously. So you will get a thick and smooth cream.

Make the cream puff on a baking pan with the help of a pastry bag.

Bake at 170° for 5 minutes, until the cream puffs swell, then lower the temperature and complete cooking.

Don't forget...

How to make cream puffs in a flash

Cocked and cooled cream puffs can be preserved empty in freezer. Ready to be defrosted and filled to taste in a few minutes, with savory (tuna, cheese or mortadella) or sweet mousses (chantilly custard, chocolate, zabaione).

You can thus organize cocktails in a very short time!

Bis cookies ✳

Ingredients and quantities for 500 g of cookies:

400 g flour
200 g sugar
80 g butter
1 dash of anise seeds
1 dash of bicarb
1 egg
2 yolks
120 g of candied, almonds, sultana, pine-nuts
white wine as needed

From a hearty tradition

Bis cookies with various flavors

The *bis* cookies can be flavored in many ways: they can be enriched with walnuts, hazelnuts, peanuts, dried plums, dates and dried figs. Their peculiar name comes from the fact they were usually made by great-grandmothers (*bisnonne*) for the whole family.

Knead 400 g of flour, 1 egg, 2 yolks, 200 g of sugar, 80 g of butter, a dash of anise seeds, one of bicarb and as much white wine as needed to make a soft and consistent mixture.

Once the mixture is well blended, make sticks of dough, lay them on a sheet of greaseproof paper and bake at 160-180° for about 15 minutes. Remove from the oven and cut 1 cm thick cookies with a knife, while they're lukewarm.

Finally, bake again and allow to toast then.

Chestnut cakes ✳ ✳

Ingredients and quantities for 6 people:

500 g chestnut flour
2 large tablespoons of dried sultana
milk as needed
fat for frying
sugar
1 large dash of bicarb
1 dash of salt

First of all, it is very important to use top quality chestnut flour.

Then, in a bowl, mix 500 g of chestnut flour and 2 large tablespoons of dried sultana, previously soaked, 1 dash of salt and a larger one of bicarb, together with the necessary milk. Blend until you get a medium consistent batter.

Plunge it into the boiling fat or oil with a tablespoons. Brown on both sides. Dry on roll paper and dust with sugar.

Castagnole ✳ ✳

> **Ingredients and quantities for 6 people:**
>
> 600 g flour
> 200 g sugar
> 4 eggs
> 130 g butter
> 1 cup of rum
> 1 cup of rosolio
> 1 sachet of chemical yeast
> fat for frying

Knead 600 g of flour, 200 g of sugar, 130 g of melted, warm butter, 1 sachet of chemical yeast, 4 yolks.

Whisk the egg-whites until stiff and add to the mix very slowly, adding 1 cup of rum. Process the mix for some time, in order to make it smooth; then, make it into 1 cm thick strings, cut them into 2 cm pieces and fry a few of them at a time in the boiling fat.

Dry the *castagnole* on roll paper, dip them in *rosolio* for a few seconds and dust with sugar.

> **The typical product of the Park**
>
> **Il marrone del Mugello**
> It differs from the chestnut because of its shape and the quality of its flesh: it is quite big and has an egg-like shape, with a sweet taste and fine flesh.
> The quality of the *marrone del Mugello* derives mainly from the way it is grown, without using fertilizers and synthetic phytosanitary products. It's rich in proteins, lipids, glucides and vitamins.
> In 1996, it has been awarded the IGP (Protected geographic indication).
> You can purchase it, every year, starting from 5th October, as a fresh or dried product (shelled or unshelled) or turned into flour.

Fried ciambelle ✳ ✳

> **Ingredients and quantities for 6 people:**
>
> 500 g flour
> 500 g boiled and mashed potatoes
> 1 egg
> 1 yolk
> 20 g brewer's yeast
> 30 g melted butter
> vanillin
> lemon and orange (grated peel)
> water as needed
> fat, a dusting of sugar

Mix 500 g of flour with 500 g of potatoes, previously boiled and mashed. Add 1 whole egg and 1 yolk, a little vanillin, 20 g of brewer's yeast, 30 g of melted butter and the grated peel of lemon and orange. Put the necessary water in the mix and blend.

Make the *ciambelle*, making horseshoe-shaped sticks of dough, joining the two ends.

Allow to rise for at least 2 hours, until they double their volume.

Fry in boiling fat or oil, dry on roll paper and dust with sugar.

Frittole ✳ ✳ ✳

Ingredients and quantities for 6 people:

400 g flour
0.5 l water
100 g butter
10 g chemical yeast
200 g soaked and dried raisins
80 g icing sugar
10 g sugar
the grated peel of 1 lemon
1 dash of vanillin
fat for frying
8 eggs
salt as needed

Heat 100 g of butter and 0.5 l of water with a little salt. When it starts boiling, pour 400 g of sifted flour.

Mix with a wooden tablespoon until you get a smooth and even mixture. Keep stirring on heat until the mixture gets thicker and detaches from the borders and from the bottom of the pan, with a little frizzling, as if frying. Then, allow to cool.

Then add 8 eggs: blend with the wooden tablespoon 1 egg at a time and add the next one only when the previous one has been completely absorbed, stirring continuously.

So you will get a thick and smooth cream. Add 10 g of chemical yeast, 200 g of soaked and dried sultana, 10 g of sugar, 1 teaspoon of grated peel of 1 lemon and 1 dash of vanillin.

Finally, plunge the mixture in the boiling fat, little by little, with a tablespoon or with a pastry bag. Then, lower the heat and fry on a medium-low heat for about 4 minutes. Dry on roll paper and dust with icing sugar.

In Venice, *frittole* are empty, in Cortina are filled with cream and pure *zabaglione*.

Mistocchine ✳

> **Ingredients and quantities for 6 people:**
>
> 500 g of chestnut flour
> 1 tablespoon of fat
> milk as needed
> 1 teaspoon of bicarb
> 10 g of salt

Prepare the mix with 500 g of chestnut flour, 10 g of salt, 1 tablespoon of fat, 1 teaspoon of bicarb and as much milk as needed. Once completely blended, make it into small balls. Flatten them a little and cook on a hot plate or in a pan.

Keep on heat for a few minutes, turning them often. Serve hot.

From a hearty tradition

In the middle of the last century, in the streets of Bologna, you could see *mistocchinaie*, ladies who made *mistocchine* and sold them to passers-by.
It was an exclusively female job. The most famous *mistocchinaia*, now in history, used to be in *via Marconi* (in the heart of the city) with her equipment for cooking.

Raviole ✳ ✳

> **Ingredients and quantities for 6 people:**
>
> for the short crust:
> 500 g flour
> 200 g sugar
> 200 g butter
> 10 g chemical yeast
> grated peel of 1 lemon
> 2 eggs
> 1 dash of salt
>
> sugar for dusting
> milk or water as needed
> fruit pickles

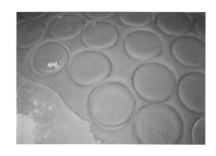

Prepare the short crust with 500 g of flour, 200 g of sugar, 200 g of butter, 2 eggs, 10 g of chemical yeast, 1 dash of salt and the grated peel of 1 lemon. Roll out the pastry, 4 mm thick.

Cut the pastry with a glass, making dishes of the desired size. The ideal diameter for a buffet is 12-13 cm. They can also be enjoyed in bigger sizes, as a snack.

Fill half of the dish with fruit pickles and close, shaping it as a half moon. Then, put the *raviole* on greaseproof paper in a baking pan.

Brush with milk or water and then dust with sugar.

Bake and cook at 180° for about 10 minutes. Remove when you see that the border is pinkish.

The *raviole* are the typical sweet of Father's day (19th March in Italy).

Fried raviole and sweet peaches ✳ ✳ ✳

Ingredients and quantities for 6-8 people:
600 g flour
200 g sugar
1 sachet of chemical yeast
130 g butter
4 eggs
oil for frying
jam
alchermes or rosolio
salt as needed

Knead 600 g of flour, 200 g of sugar, 1 sachet of chemical yeast, 130 g of flavored butter and salt. Then, make a well and add 4 eggs. Process until you get a very soft dough. The dough of *raviole* is very difficult to roll out: the ideal way is to roll it on greaseproof paper or on a marble surface, and process it with the help of a palette knife.

Roll out the pastry, cut with a glass in the shape of a dish and fill with jam.

Close in the shape of a half moon and plunge in boiling oil until they're golden.

Lay on roll paper, dip in alchermes or *rosolio* and then dust with sugar. The jam filling can also be replaced with custard.

The same process can be used to make the so-called sweet peaches. Use the same dough to make small balls, then press them on their base and cut them to shape them like a peach.

Bake at 160° for 15-20 minutes. Remove from the oven and allow to cool.

Fill the two halves with chocolate or jam and join them, making a whole peach. Dip in alchermes and dust with sugar.

Sfrappole ✳ ✳ ✳

Ingredients and quantities for 4 people:

260 g flour
1 egg
15 g cognac or brandy
0.5 dl orange juice
10 g butter
8 g icing sugar
fat or seed oil for frying
vanilla sugar
salt as needed

Prepare the mix blending 1 egg, 260 g of flour, 15 g of cognac or brandy, 0,5 room orange juice, 10 g of butter, 8 g of icing sugar and 1 dash of salt, trying to make a soft mixture.

Lay a pastry even thinner than that used for *tortellini* (the right thickness is achieved by very expert *sfoglini*). Use a pastry cutter to cut strips, at least 4 cm wide and 15 cm long. Then, make them into knots.

Fry into the boiling fat or oil, moving them quickly. Once they are golden, strain and dry with roll paper.

Lay on a serving dish and dust with vanilla sugar, adding it slowly.

From a hearty tradition

The Epiphany lunch has always been seen as the last holiday connected with Christmas. For this reason, it was never characterized by a special dish.

Many families preferred to use that day to close the Christmas holidays and start the Carnival celebrations. Thus, at the end of the lunch, they gladly served some "advance" *sfrappole*, sided by a sweet wine.

Fried tagliatelle ✳ ✳

Ingredients and quantities for 6 people:

for the dough:
500 g flour
4 eggs
30 g cognac or brandy
orange juice as needed
10 g butter
1 tablespoon of icing sugar

grated peel of 1 lemon
fat for frying
a dusting of sugar
a dusting of vanilla sugar
salt as needed

Knead 4 eggs, 500 g of flour, 30 g of cognac or brandy, 1 tablespoon of icing sugar, 10 g of butter and as much orange juice as you need in order to knead. Blend the ingredients well.

Roll out a medium thick pastry and allow to dry. Dust with abundant sugar and the grated peel of 1 lemon. Cut the *tagliatelle* into rolls, as described in the traditional *tagliatelle* recipe (see page 23), without opening the "nests".

Plunge the *tagliatelle* nests in the boiling fat, so that the surface sugar caramelizes and the *tagliatelle* get cooked.

Some *tagliatelle* open while cooking, some others stay closed, but this is the characteristics of this sweet.

Dust with vanilla sugar and serve.

Fried tortelloni ✲ ✲

Ingredients and quantities for 6 people:

for the dough:
500 g flour
30 g cognac or brandy
orange juice as needed
2 eggs
20 g butter
salt as needed

for the yellow cream:
50 g flour
0.5 l milk
150 g sugar
2 eggs
grated peel of 1 lemon
fat for frying
1 dash of salt

Prepare the dough for *tortelloni* with 2 eggs, 500 g of flour, 20 g of butter, 30 g of cognac or brandy and 1 dash of salt. Blend and then add as much orange juice as needed to make the dough compact.

Prepare the cream with 3 eggs, 0,5 l of milk, 50 g of flour, sugar, the grated peel of 1 lemon and 1 dash of salt.

Roll out a not very thin pastry and prepare the *tortelloni*, filling them with the yellow cream, then fry them in boiling fat. Strain, dry on roll paper and dust with vanilla sugar before serving.

Anise sugarplums ✲ ✲ ✲

Ingredients and quantities for 6 people:

350 g flour
130 g sugar
1 tablespoon of milk
1 tablespoon seed oil
a spray of sassolino
10 g powder yeast
2 eggs

for the frosting:
1/2 glass of anise
250 g sugar
0,7 dl water
1 pinch of anise seeds

Prepare the mix for sugarplums, blending 2 eggs, 130 g of sugar, 1 tablespoon of milk, 350 g of flour and 10 g of powder yeast. Once you have a smooth and soft mixture, make it into rings, thinner than 1 cm. Put them on greaseproof paper in a baking tin and bake at 180° for about 10 minutes. Cook carefully, because the sugarplums are ready even if they stay soft.

Allow to rest even a whole night.

Prepare a bottle of frosting with 75 g water, 250 g of sugar, 1/2 glass of anise and 1 dash of anise seeds. Proceed to frosting the following day.

Cook the frosting in a pan, on a high heat and allow to become dense. Add the sugarplums little by little.

Turn the sugarplums often while frosting. Lay them on a platter and allow to cool. Then serve.

Fruit in syrup and jams, liquors and hot beverages

And now some fruit… Apricots, peaches, cherries and marasca cherries in alcohol and even frigs in balsamic vinegar, or caramelized fruit. Many dishes to end a meal, tasty and based on fruit, enriched with syrup or red wine. Candied flavors for cakes and jams that can be fabulously sided by cheeses.

You will also find the traditional liquors: with egg or coffee, walnuts and *rosolio*. If you want to fight the cold winter, on the other hand, we suggest a glass of orange or tangerine punch or mulled wine.

Finally, all the secrets for preparing a quick and delicious hot chocolate!

Balsamic figs ✳

Ingredients:

fichi
aceto balsamico
zucchero semolato

It is better to choose very small and solid figs, red or black. Wash and allow to dry. Fill some jars, trying to optimize the space: the first layer of figs with their tips upwards, the second layer upside down, and so on.

Cover with sugar up to 2 cm from the border of the jar. At this point, add 1 teaspoon of balsamic vinegar.

Seal and leave in the cellar for at least 3-4 months.

The balsamic figs can be served with or without cheese. They are perfect to end a meal.

History has it that in the past centuries balsamic vinegar, a vinegar-based condiment having healing properties, used to be served as a *cordiale*, at the end of the meal.

The typical product of the Park

Pecorino reggiano cheese
More than 15.000 sheep graze in the National Parc of Appennino Tosco-Emiliano. Most of them belong to the *massese* race.
From their milk, mostly mixed with cow milk, originate cheeses which don't ripen for more than one or two months. Among these, the pecorino reggiano, which due to its limited maturing is not suitable for grating. You can serve it with figs and balsamic vinegar, or with jams.

Candied fruit ✳

Ingredients :

orange peels
citron peels
figs
cherries
chestnuts

for the syrup:
1 l water
800 g sugar

for the caramel:
sugar
water

Candied orange and citron: first of all, chop the orange peels and remove the white part completely. Then chop the citron peels, leaving some of the white part.

Meanwhile, prepare the syrup with 1 l of water and 800 g of sugar. When it starts boiling, add the peels of both fruits and allow to cook in the syrup for a few minutes.

Remove after 8-10 minutes and allow to cool, well lain, for about half an hour.

Finally, repeat the process, plunging the orange and citron peels in the syrup one more time. Turn off heat and allow to rest in the hot syrup.

Candied figs and cherries: follow the above mentioned cooking method and repeat three times.

Marron glacé: it is necessary to repeat the same process four times.

Finally, after making the various kinds of candied fruit, put them on a platter to dry.

Figs jam ✳

Ingredients and quantities for 1 kg of jam:

1 kg figs
500 g sugar

The best period to make the figs jam is in July or August. Choose not very ripe figs, possibly round and small, especially the sweetest ones.

Weight the figs with their peel, wash and cut them into two halves or segments. Cook 1 kg of figs and 500 g of sugar on a low heat in an aluminum, earthenware, or enamel pan. Never use a stainless steel pan. Stir continuously until you get the right consistency of the jam. Fill some jars and boil in a bain-marie for 20 minutes.

Figs jam is perfect with *ricotta* or *mascarpone* cheese, also sided by *piadine* and *crescentine*.

Fruit pickles ✻

Ingredients and quantities for 1 kg of fruit pickles:

1 kg quinces
150 g non-ripe pears
250 g dried plums
50 g shelled almonds
100 g sultana
0.5 dl water
500 g of sugar
grated peel of 1 lemon
1 cm of cinnamon stick
2 tablespoons vinegar
1 teaspoon of grains of mustard

Dice 1 kg of quinces and 150 g of pears, without peeling them and removing the cores. Add 250 g of dried plums, 50 g of shelled almonds, 100 g sultana, the grated peel of 1 lemon, 1 cm of cinnamon stick, 2 tablespoons of vinegar, 1 teaspoon of grains of mustard, 0.5 l of water and 500 g of sugar. Cook all the ingredients together and turn off heat when the quinces are ready. Then process with a vegetable mill.

Fill the jars and cook in a bain-marie for 30 minutes.

From a hearty tradition

Both fruit pickles and figs jam can be considered as "born out of necessity".

Quinces, which are the main ingredient of fruit pickles, cannot be eaten raw: in the past, they were processed in a jam to use them as edible food.

Figs, fresh and ripe, could be spoilt in just a day (if not stored in modern fridges!): either you ate them when harvested or you had to throw them away.

Turning them into a jam allowed to save this fruit.

Pears, apples and plums in red wine ✻ ✻

Ingredients and quantities for 6 people:

6 pears or 6 apples or 18 plums
1 l red wine
grated peel of 1 lemon
some cloves
sugar

Choose among pears, apples and plums and proceed according to the following instructions.

Apples-pears: cut them into halves without peeling them, removing the bottom footstalk. Wash and put in a large pan. Cover with red wine, add the grated peel of 1 lemon and some cloves. Dust with sugar, cover the pan with a lid and boil on a medium-high heat for 10 minutes.

Plums: leave them whole. Plums should be put in infusion the night before, covered with red boil wine. Allow to rest the whole night. The next day, put them back on heat with the peel of 1 lemon and some cloves. Dust with sugar and cover with a lid. Serve after 5 minutes from the boiling point. Serve immediately.

Peaches, apricots, cherries and marasca cherries in alcohol ✻

for the syrup:
1 l water
500 g sugar (for the cherries, 450 g)
grated peel of 1 lemon
peaches
apricots
cherries
marasca cherries

Peaches and apricots: firstly, prepare the syrup with 1 l of water, 500 g of sugar and just the yellow part of a lemon's peel (2 cm).

Boil sugar with water for 5 minutes and skim (if it foams, due to sugar being more refined today); turn off heat and allow to cool.

Choose yellow peaches, with a big pit well separated from the flesh. Wash and discard those that are too ripe.

Plunge in boiling water and remove immediately, so that you can peel them better. Cut them into two halves, removing the pit. Fill the jars, pressing the peaches one on the other, up to 2 cm from the jar's mouth.

Cover with syrup, close the jars and cook in a bain-marie for about 10 minutes. If peaches are big allow 12-13 minutes.

Choose almost unripe apricots, yellow.

Wash and cut them into two halves, removing the pit. Fill the jars, removing the air as for peaches, cover with syrup. Boil in a bain-marie for 3 minutes.

Cherries or marasca cherries: prepare the syrup, decreasing the quantity of sugar. Thus, boil 1 l of water with 450 g of sugar. Or keep the same quantity of sugar and add 1 glass of water.

Choose big cherries only. Wash and cut them into two halves, removing the pit. Marasca cherries are left whole.

Fill the jars, cover with syrup and boil in a bain-marie for 4-5 minutes.

Don't forget...

Storing syrup
It is advisable to prepare syrup and store it in a bottle.
We suggest boiling even 10-15 l of syrup at a time.

Alchermes *

Ingredients and quantities for 3 bottles:

0.75 l water
1200 g sugar
7 dl of alcohol 70%
flavors: nutmeg, cloves, rose or orange blossoms water, cinnamon

Prepare the syrup with 0.75 l of water and 1200 g of sugar, or use leftover syrup of fruit in syrup, as long as you have about 2 l of syrup.

Then, add 7 dl of alcohol and the flavors: nutmeg, cloves, rose or orange blossoms water, cinnamon.

Make an infusion at least 10 days before and then sift.

The liquor can be served only after 30 days.

Hot chocolate *

Ingredients and quantities for each cup:

1 tablespoon of sugared cocoa
1 teaspoon of starch
milk as needed

or
icing sugar
bitter cocoa
starch
milk

Melt 1 tablespoon of sugared cocoa and 1 table-spoon of starch with cold milk. Stir on heat, until the chocolate is thick.

You can also make hot chocolate with bitter cocoa, mixing 100 g of icing sugar and 100 g of bitter cocoa. Mix and then use 1 level tablespoon per cup. Finally, add 1 teaspoon of starch and boil with milk.

According to personal taste, you can increase or decrease the quantity of starch, depending on if you like your chocolate to be more or less thick.

Coffee liquor *

Ingredients and quantities for 2 bottles:

1 l coffee
200 g sugar
250 g alcohol 70%

On heat, mix 1 l of coffee, 200 g of sugar and 250 g of alcohol 70%. The liquor is ready when it boils. Allow to cool and store in the fridge for at least 15 days before serving.

Egg liquor ✳

Ingredients and quantities for 2 bottles:

1 l milk
400 g sugar
100 g marsala
100 g alcohol 70%
4 eggs

Mix 4 eggs, 400 g of sugar, 100 g of marsala and 100 g alcohol. Blend with care and add 1 l of milk. Leave it in infusion for 2 days. Sift and bottle.

The egg liquor can be served after about 20 days. Store in fridge exclusively.

Nocino (Walnut liquor) ✳

Ingredients and quantities for 2 bottles:

25 walnuts
1 l alcohol
500 g sugar
4 dl water
2 lemons peel
6 cloves
2 pinches of cinnamon

Walnuts are harvested between 15th and 23rd June, and that's exactly the best period to make *nocino*. Check the right ripening state of walnuts by piercing them with a toothpick: if it pierces through, they can be harvested.

Prepare a syrup boiling 4 dl of water and 500 g of sugar. Allow to cool. At this point, add 1 l alcohol, 25 walnuts cut into halves or segments and 2 lemons peel. Add the flavors: 5 cloves and 1 dash of cinnamon. Leave it in infusion at room temperature for 40 days.

Sift and allow to rest in a cellar until December (it must be a fresh place, far from the light, better in a demijohn).

Bottle in December and serve around Christmas.

Orange or tangerine punch *

> **Ingredients and quantities for 1 bottle:**
>
> 250 g rum
> 1.7 dl alcohol 70%
> 1.7 dl water
> 170 g sugar
> juice of an orange or a tangerine
> peel of an orange or a tangerine
> peel of 1 lemon

Prepare the syrup boiling 1.7 dl of water and 170 g of sugar. Add 1.70 of alcohol and 250 g of rum. Then add the juice of an orange or a tangerine and its peel. Leave it in infusion for 3 days.

Sift and pour in dark bottles. Serve after a month.

Rose rosolio *

> **Ingredients and quantities for 3 bottles:**
>
> 1 kg sugar
> 500 g rose petals
> 05 l water
> juice of 1 lemon
> 500 g alcohol 70%

Prepare the syrup boiling 0.5 l of water and 1 kg of sugar. When hot, add 500 g of rose petals and the juice of 1 lemon. Allow to cool and add 500 g of alcohol 70%.

Leave it in infusion for 48 hours. Sift and bottle. Serve after 30 days.

Mulled wine ✳

Ingredients and quantities for 1 glass:

1 and 1/2 glass of red wine
1 level tablespoon of sugar
2 cloves
1/2 cm cinnamon stick
1 lemon peel
brandy (as desired)

Mulled wine must be made with a good red wine.

Mix 1 glass and 1/2 of red wine with 1 level table-spoon of sugar, 2 clove, 1/2 cm of cinnamon stick and 1 lemon peel. Boil until the alcohol evaporates. Sometimes it flames … but not always. However, boil it for 10 minutes. As desired, enrich with a spray of liquor (brandy).

Finally sift and serve hot.

In winter nights, it is perfectly sided by cookies or roast chestnuts.

Alfabetical index of the recipes

A

Alchermes – 195
Almond cake – 173
Anise sugarplums – 189
Apple and nut ciambella – 163
Apple pie – 174
Artichokes casserole – 127

B

Baked onions – 129
Balanzoni – 24
Balanzoni with butter
and sage sauce – 67
Balsamic figs – 191
Barilino – 30
Bean soup – 106
Béchamel sauce – 90
Béchamel sauce with eggs – 91
Bis cookies – 182
Bitter-sweet baby onions – 130
Bolognese cutlets – 116
Bolognese meat-sauce – 94
Bolognese sauce lasagne – 69
Bread dough: type 1 or mix to make
"mother" yeast – 28
Bread dough: type 2 – 29
Bread shapes – 30
Breadsticks – 31
Butter and cinnamon seasoning – 92
Butter and gold sauce – 92

C

Candied fruit – 192
Cannelloni Gratin – 68
Caramelle – 24
Carciofo – 30
Carrot cake – 170
Castagnole – 183
Certosino or pan speziale – 160
Cestini – 24

Cheese and basil sauce – 92
Cheese mousse – 62
Chestnut cakes – 182
Chicken cacciatore – 120
Chocolate cake – 171
Chocolate ice-cream – 151
Chocolate mousse – 154
Chocolate pudding – 149
Chocolate sauce – 155
Ciambella or brazadèla – 162
Ciribusla or bean
and polenta soup – 107
Clams sauce – 103
Classic polenta – 40
Coffee liquor – 196
Coffee pudding – 148
Cream puffs – 181
Crème caramel – 150
Crocetta or nodino – 31
Custard cake – 172

D

Dried salt cod with milk – 142

E

Easter Ciambella – 161
Egg liquor – 197
Eggplants Parmigiana – 132
Eggs with spinach – 139
English custard – 150
Erbazzone – 53

F

Figs jam – 192
Filled peppers – 134
Fior di latte – 152
Flavored butter seasoning – 91
Fried cardoons – 127
Fried ciambelle – 183
Fried crescentine – 52

Fried custard – 37
Fried fruit – 39
Fried lamb ribs – 116
Fried polenta – 40
Fried raviole
and sweet peaches – 186
Fried tagliatelle – 188
Fried tortelloni – 189
Friggione – 131
Frittole – 184
Fruit pickles – 193

G
Galantine or rifreddo – 54
Garganelli – 19
Garlic and parsley straccetti – 81
Giblets meat-sauce – 99
Gnocchi – 19
Gorgonzola cheese sauce – 100
Grandma Carla's meatballs – 121
Granita – 152
Gratin of cardoons – 128
Gratin of fennels – 130
Gratin of tomatoes – 135
Grattini – 21
Green sauce for mixed boiled
meat – 103

H
Ham meat-sauce – 98
Herring in oil or "gracious" herring – 142
Hot chocolate – 196
Hot sauce for mixed boiled meat – 101

I
Imperial soup – 112
Italian custard – 149

L
Lasagne with angler and shrimps – 72
Lasagne with artichokes – 70
Lettuce Ravioli – 74
Loaf – 31

M
Maccheroni and peas pie – 73
Malfattini – 21
Maltagliati – 21
Mascarpone – 153
Mash potatoes – 136
Mature cheese – 145
Meat loaf – 123
Meat or fish flan – 61
Meat pie – 118
Meringue – 165
Mezzelune – 25
Milk pork chops – 115
Minestrone – 108
Mistocchine – 185
Mixed boiled meats – 114
Mixed pickled vegetables – 56
Montebianco – 166
Mortadella cutlets – 117
Mortadella mousse – 63
Mulled wine – 199
Mushroom sauce – 96

N
Nocino (Walnut liquor) – 197
Nutella (chocolate spread)
and cream cake – 175

O
Onion pie – 64
Orange or tangerine punch – 198

P
Pan roast chicken, guinea-fowl or
rabbit – 120
Pannacotta (Cooked cream) – 154
Panone – 167
Parpadellini or quadretti – 21
Parpadellini with peas – 110
Passatelli – 111
Peaches, apricots, cherries and
marasca cherries in alcohol – 194
Pears, apples and plums
in red wine – 194

Peas and ham meat-sauce – 97
Peas and meatballs – 122
Peas meat-sauce – 97
Peas with ham – 135
Piadina – 57
Pickled baby onions – 51
Pickled vegetable
or baby artichoke butter – 51
Pineapple cake – 170
Pinza – 168
Polenta – 40
Polenta with dried salt cod – 49
Polenta with duck – 44
Polenta with guinea-hen – 48
Polenta with hare – 46
Polenta with pheasant – 42
Polenta with pork spare ribs – 44
Polenta with rabbit
or chicken cacciatore – 45
Polenta with sausage sauce – 41
Pollicioni – 25
Porcini mushrooms filling – 138
Porcini mushrooms sauce – 104
Potato and meat ravioli – 76
Potato filling – 86
Potato pie – 119
Potato roll – 137
Pumpkin Tortelloni – 84

Q
Quiche Lorraine – 58

R
Radicchio filling – 86
Radicchio and pine-nuts
filling – 137
Raviole – 185
Ravioli – 25
Red lasagne with cheeses – 71
Red turnip ravioli – 75
Rice cake or torta
degli addobbi – 176
Ricotta and fruit tart – 163
Ricotta and spinach sauce – 98

Ricotta tortelloni – 83
Ricotta – 146
Roast pork – 113
Roast veal – 114
Rocket filling – 85
Rolled omelette – 54
Rose rosolio – 198

S
Saint Petronius' bread – 32
Saint-Honoré cake – 179
Salmon sauce – 101
Salmon tortelli – 82
Sausage meat-sauce – 100
Sausage mix – 94
Savoury pie – 65
Savoy filling – 87
Semolina fritters – 38
Sfilzini – 59
Sfrappole – 187
Sherbet – 156
Soft cheese – 144
Sole-fish ravioli – 77
Soup in a sack – 107
Spareribs – 124
Spinach filling – 138
Spinach roll – 77
Sponge cake – 166
Stew – 123
Stewed cardoons – 129
Stewed eel – 141
Stewed eggs – 139
Stock – 105
Strawberry Bavarian cream – 147
Strawberry cake – 169
Strichetti or farfalle – 19
Stringy potatoes – 133
Strozzapreti – 22
Stuffed crescenta
with ciccioli or onion – 52
Stuffed zucchini – 126
Sweet filling – 88

T

Tagliatelle Bolognese – 78
Tagliatelle cake – 176
Taglioline with salmon – 79
Three-color tortellacci – 79
Tigelle – 64
Tiramisù – 157
Toasted polenta with cheeses – 41
Tomato soup with straccetti – 109
Torta margherita – 177
Torta sabbiosa (Sandy cake) – 178
Torta sbrisolona (Crumbly cake) – 180
Tortellacci – 27
Tortellini – 26
Tortellini in stock – 111
Tortelloni – 27
Triangoli – 25
Truffle butter – 51
Truffled tortelloni – 83
Tuna butter – 50
Tuna loaf – 143
Tuna mousse – 63
Two-color ciambella – 164

V

Vanilla Bavarian cream – 147
Vanilla ice-cream – 151
Veal with tuna sauce – 125
Vegetable filling – 87
Vegetable flan – 61
Vegetable fritters – 132
Vegetable sauce – 102

W

Walnut cake – 174
Walnut filling – 85
Walnut soufflé – 157
Whipped zabaglione – 158
White flan with giblet meat sauce – 60

Y

Yogurt cake – 172

Z

Zucchini and shrimp sauce – 93
Zucchini pie – 66
Zuppa inglese (English trifle) – 158

Printed in Italy
by Grafiche Damiani (BO)
October 2004